MASTERING
THE
CHALLENGES
OF
CHANGE

MASTERING

THE

CHALLENGES

OF

CHANGE

Strategies for
Each Stage in
Your Organization's
Life Cycle

LeRoy Thompson, Jr.

amacom

American Management Association

New York • Atlanta • Boston • Chicago • Kansas City • San Francisco • Washington, D.C.
Brussels • Mexico City • Tokyo • Toronto

Library of Congress Cataloging-in-Publication Data

Thompson, LeRoy, 1954–
    Mastering the challenges of change : strategies for each stage in
your organization's life cycle / LeRoy Thompson, Jr.
     p.   cm.
    Includes index.
    ISBN 0-8144-0218-6
    1. Organizational change.   I. Title:
HD58.8.T49   1994
658.4′063—dc20
                                      94-28683
                                         CIP

Printing number
10 9 8 7 6 5 4 3 2 1

This book is
dedicated to my father,
LeRoy Thompson, Sr.,
who set an easy-to-follow
example of compassion and courage.

Contents

Preface

Those of us in positions of leadership recognize that the most dependable organizational phenomenon is change. Either we seek to induce change because it is necessary for growth and prosperity or we must scurry about to handle its effects, because change has the power to derail our progress. In either case two critical skills are required. First, we must be able to identify where the organization is and what needs to be done to maximize its capabilities. Second, we must be able to figure out where we need to go and to lead others through the process of adjusting, adapting, and ultimately embracing a new method, a new procedure, a new policy, or a new way of thinking.

This book will provide you with those skills and may even increase your appetite for taking on these challenges. To begin, we'll cover the principles of the relationship of change to the organization's culture, as well as how change can affect an entire industry or sector. Then we will trace the stages of organizational change, identifying the appropriate management tools in each stage. In the final chapter we will come full circle and discuss skills for and insights into dealing with the nitty-gritty interpersonal issues.

I have set out to make three particular contributions to this important topic. The first is to help you avoid fads in management and organizational development. It seems that people grab on to the latest idea—strategic planning, TQM, customer service, empowerment, cultural diversity—and launch headlong into some sort of program. This creates a lot of instability for the employees and, worse yet, can hurt the credibility of the idea if the timing or situation isn't right. I hope to give you some knowledge of how to use each of these ideas and the wisdom to know which one is most appropriate for your situation.

The second contribution is to integrate the notion of leadership into the handling of change. While the importance of management and supervisory skills has always been emphasized, it is only in the last few years that business leaders have come to grips with the fact that those skills alone are insufficient. Maintaining commitment and morale in the face of the change issues that most organizations will continue to confront requires a degree of care and concern for the welfare of human beings that goes far beyond just managing and supervising. In addition, the barriers between levels, functions, and categories of employees will become increasingly more unproductive. We will all have to learn to collaborate in creating a work climate that is both conducive to responding to the needs of customers and clients and flexible enough to address new concepts of getting the job done. Chapter 7 addresses the organizational stage-specific priority of leadership skills, but the deeper principles of creating the proper climate for human beings to function effectively in will be a recurring theme throughout the book.

The third, and perhaps most significant, contribution is that I have tried to simplify the ideas and techniques so that you can readily incorporate them into your change management practices and leadership strategies. The goal is not to downplay the complexity of the issues, but to carve these ideas into manageable pieces that don't require much translation for you to see benefits. While the analysis of the stages of change can be done in a much more sophisticated fashion, my framework should be more usable. It will enable you to ask the right questions to use those techniques more effectively and with a greater pay-off.

Acknowledgments

Special thanks to . . .

My wife Rita, my daughter Aisha, and my son Lee for giving me time, space, encouragement, and affirmation.

My mom, Mentora Thompson, for the lessons she continues to teach me on managing change with dignity and optimism.

Adrienne Hickey at AMACOM for her incredible patience, wisdom, and ability to give honest and direct feedback.

Pastors Cameron and Anna Simmons for their prayers, encouragement, and unfailing faith.

Priscilla Cuddy and Michael (Doc) Doran of Legacy Management Associates for lessons learned in the client laboratory and in our many airport brainstorming sessions.

T. Quinn Spitzer and Dr. Ron Evans of Kepner-Tregoe for teaching me everything I know about organizational development.

The personnel of the many client organizations who gave unselfishly their time in interviews, their data and information, and their research.

One

Understanding Change

While theoretically and technically television may be feasible, commercially and financially I consider it an impossibility, a development of which we need waste little time dreaming.

—*Lee De Forest, American Inventor (1873–1961)*

Ever notice how well-organized and structured everything appears when you look at the world from the window of an airplane? When you're still on the ground, the close proximity to the scene gives you a perspective that often highlights the chaos and disorder. This book will enable leaders to see organizational change from the "airplane" perspective and equip them with the concepts and techniques necessary to manage it more effectively. By understanding the nature and dynamics of organizational change, they will then be able to channel the natural resistance from employees into productive momentum toward accomplishing the mission of the organization. The book will provide answers to the perplexing questions of organizational change and present commonsense tools for analyzing complex issues:

- What major sources of change are shaping our environment?

- Do organizations go through predictable phases of growth and crisis?
- Can you really be proactive and anticipate change?
- Are strategic planning and total quality management more than just buzzwords?
- How do you make the "customer-focus" concept operational?
- What is leadership? Is it different from management?
- How do you involve employees without losing control?
- When does resistance turn into mutiny?

The Lay of the Land

The true sign of intelligence is the ability to hold two contradictory thoughts in one's mind at the same time.
—*Isaac Asimov*

At first glance Asimov's statement may be a bit perplexing, but if you give it some time, it'll sink in. It certainly has for me. As I have watched and participated with thousands of executives and managers in dealing with the impact of change on their organizations, I have noticed that what separates the successful from the less fortunate is not an abundance of resources, a competitive advantage, or more experience. No, it's far simpler than that. It's a state of mind, a posture, a certain perspective that gives an organization's leaders the ability to see the silver lining in the clouds and convince everyone around them that it's there.

Those who can understand that threat *and* opportunity, risk *and* benefit, as well as countless other environmental paradoxes, can exist simultaneously will tend to be the best equipped to guide others through the perils of this new order of management and organizational reality. Change is nothing new, yet it seems to be having a debilitating impact on the quality of management. Sensitivity to demographic shifts, rapid advances in technology, and major alterations in cultural values have compounded the task of producing results through other people.

"Consider Your Ways"

Perhaps *debilitating impact* seems a bit strong; nevertheless, it has become painfully obvious that we are in serious trouble. Many of the ills that plague us, though, aren't really the fault of people but more so their unfortunate reactions and responses to organizational systems that are badly out of whack. In fact, while people do act a bit like lemmings and pursue their hopeless ends with misplaced zeal (or, worse yet, act like slaughterhouse sheep buying into their fate believing they have no recourse), most I have interacted with are doing the best they can. Yet that doesn't excuse the fact that there are problems, and if they're not addressed, the winds of change will sweep business, government, and even some of our nonprofit organizations under the rug. Our organizations lack vision, have become inwardly focused, and have lost contact with customers and employees alike. We've simply got to "consider our ways" as the Old Testament prophet Haggai, warned.

Three major obstacles seem to stand in the way of our ability to apply a conscious introspective approach: (1) our inherent, almost biochemical reaction to change itself, (2) the short-term mentality that seems to permeate the environment of most organizations in our culture, and (3) the need to rethink the criteria used to measure success.

The Reality of Resistance to Change

I've discovered that nobody really likes change. Variety is fine, but real, honest-to-goodness change is something else. In fact, most change may even be counterintuitive, in that it goes against the basic survival instinct of an individual (and hence a group, as in an organization). This all sounds quite understandable, but the implications of resisting change are quite serious.

People in management talk a lot about change. They preach about how this new program or that new concept will make things "different around here," but in truth they have no heartfelt desire to make anything different. They ask, directly or indirectly, for greater levels of commitment and convince at least the newer members of the organization that they are sincere in their advocating of new ideas and their embracing of change. But making promises and not keeping them is one of the most demoralizing experiences for human beings. It robs them of hope and activates a defense mechanism that imperils the achieving of any kind of satisfactory job performance. After years of talk but no appreciable change, apathy and cynicism become the accepted attitude. And worse yet it becomes contagious. If you analyzed how things were going in your organization and found that even the newer people were jaded about the prospects of positive change, that should tell you a lot about how far this cancer had spread.

Most behavioral scientists would agree that in any organization that finds itself crippled by problems associated with change, the search for solutions begins at the top, with those who have the authority to make adjustments in direction and methodology.

The Curse of Short-Term Thinking

Another factor that I have seen play a major role in hampering the ability to manage organizational change is the short-term mentality that predominates in organizational life. To gain the proper perspective on change requires that we see the big picture. Well, it seems that over the last forty years or so, our time horizons have gotten shorter and shorter. Corporations now measure their revenues and earnings per share at least every three months, nonprofits conduct fund-raising campaigns and gauge their success on the numbers of dollars and volunteers they can muster, churches look at the membership rolls and tithing records, and government organizations look at the negativity of media coverage or attendance at public hearings.

Each of these ways of determining how well we're doing

has validity. The problem is that for a lot of organizations, these have become the benchmarks of their strategy for dealing with the future. As much as earnings per share or media coverage may tell us that we are doing things right, it doesn't give any indication of whether we are doing the *right* things. If the numbers are good, we get lulled into a false sense of security, and if they are bad, we put more pressure on our people to generate them. Either way we miss the boat.

Rethinking How We Measure Success

To deal with change effectively, we need to look at the longer-term issues that may dictate where we should be headed and what approaches we should take to get there. In an environment characterized by change, the role of managers is first to create a compelling sense of direction, which employees embrace, and then to evaluate continuously the way we do things to stay in step with the needs of those we are doing the work for. The problem is that performance measures give us little insight into success. Rather, they lead us to and settle for near-term benefits, often at the expense of the longer-run vitality of the organization. They will not provoke us to consider improving the systems and procedures that touch our customers, clients, or employees or lead us to feel that the investment of time and energy to make these improvements is worth it.

You know the rest of the story. Even well-regarded and highly successful institutions gradually lose contact with those they serve. Then the context within which they provide services begins to change, almost imperceptibly. At some point they go out of business or, worse, hang on while suboptimizing shareholders' wealth, eroding the confidence of the public, and frustrating their employees, staff, or volunteers beyond repair. Whether it's Conrail, W.T. Grant, or the Franklin National Bank, the pattern leading toward obsolescence is the same.

Figure 1-1. Stages of organizational change.

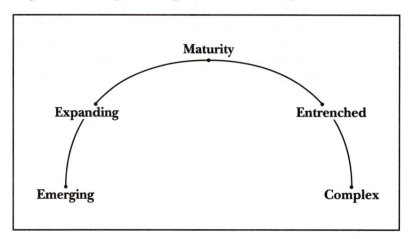

Times and Seasons

Every living thing operates on the basis of some sort of cycle, and it's useful to view organizations in this way too. Organizations seem to pass through distinct phases over time, and each stage of change creates a very different organizational culture. Figure 1-1 shows these stages.

This is the framework that we will use in examining change throughout the remainder of the book. The key to effectiveness is to know the dynamics of the stage that you are in and what concepts and techniques will make the best contribution toward achieving the mission of your organization. In reality, each of these five stages is likely to have several variations on the main theme. For practical purposes each presents clear challenges and goals.

In the Emerging stage, the challenge is to establish a clear direction in order to guide the decisions that will ultimately shape the organization's future. The goal is to create a clear picture of where the organization should be headed, what specific things it needs to accomplish to fulfill its mission, and how it intends to go about implementing the mission.

In the Expanding stage, the challenge is to make continuous improvements in methods and procedures. The key to effectiveness is decreasing the cost of operations while maintaining a high quality of product/service delivery. The goal is to make sure that the expectations of that delivery are understood and that the processes are appropriate.

The Maturity stage presents the challenge of avoiding (or repairing) the loss of contact with customers or constituents that can be a natural consequence of growth and expansion. This loss of contact necessitates that the organization develop ways to learn the wants and needs of the users of their products and services and to make sure that the systems and processes continue to deliver on the basis of those wants and needs.

The Entrenched stage is perhaps the most challenging of all. The organization still remains a viable entity but has lost the energy that had been responsible for innovations in meeting the needs of customers and constituents. Barriers between departments and functions now make even routine collaboration cumbersome, if not impossible. The goal is to make the concept of empowerment a practical element of the organization's culture.

In the Complex stage, the challenge is that the organization in its present mode of operating is not a viable entity in the long term. Sometimes the decay is so acute that short-term viability is threatened and there is a need to recreate the framework of what is really a new entity. In many respects this brings us full circle to the goals of the Emerging organization and the priority of a new vision for a new future.

This way of looking at change—its stages and the organizational cultures that flow from those stages—will be our cornerstone.

Goals, Needs, and Critical Issues

Figure 1-2 summarizes the salient features of this approach to looking at the stages of organizational change. Since the overall schematic really represents a continuum of change,

Figure 1-2. Aspects of the stages of organizational change.

Stage	Operational Goal	Organizational Priority	Change Management Issues
Emerging	Resources for growth	Direction	Clear focus of future nature and direction
Expanding	Return on investment	Execution	Effective processes and systems
Maturity	Product/ market position	Sensitivity	Ability to attract and hold to customers
Entrenched	Innovation	Leadership	Creation of opportunities for creativity
Complex	Diversification	Recreation	Challenge historic assumptions

the key is to understand the goals, priorities, and critical issues that the organization is confronted with. But this is only the macro side of change. We need to take a quick look at the micro side as well—the tools and insights that are needed to give us a solid foundation and the proper perspective on change.

The Emerging Stage

The **Emerging** organization isn't necessarily a start-up venture, although that's the example that's easiest to grasp. At this stage, the opportunities outweigh the capacities, and decisions are driven by the immediacy of those opportunities. It is not yet time to think of planning or other formal procedures.

There is a desperate need for someone (or something) to help establish clarity in the organization's direction. Management is required to direct the acquisition of resources and the placement of them toward accomplishing whatever the business objectives are understood to be. The pitfalls of this stage are obvious, and a number of organizations have failed as a result: they have succeeded too quickly and lack the infrastructure to sustain the momentum. You probably have been close to an entrepreneur whose widget worked wonders in the marketplace, but as the business began to explode, the lack of sales, marketing, accounting, bookkeeping, and other essential but basic management skills became a liability. Even older, more established entities can experience the Emerging stage.

Consider AT&T's Universal Card unit, which won the 1992 Malcolm Baldrige National Quality Award. As an emerging operation, the Universal Card went out of its way with a strategy to deliver the type of customer service considered unnecessary by the competition, giving the fledgling operation a flood of new opportunities to penetrate the market for low-interest credit cards.

You can also observe trends of emergence in new approaches or strategies to existing operations. For example, you can expect to see everyone from your neighborhood food and consumer goods company to your local charity capitalizing on the trend of more men performing household chores.

This new focus will create avenues in marketing and product development just as the graying of our society has done with an increased emphasis on the needs of the elderly.

You'll witness the same organizational change issue of priority in the clarity of strategic direction in the area of emerging technology. Recently the pharmaceutical companies have unlocked the potential of the chemical serotonin, which the circulatory system uses to constrict blood vessels and occurs naturally in the human brain. New businesses that seek to produce derivatives of the chemical to treat everything from headaches to heart disease will likely behave much like the entrepreneur with his widget.

The Expanding Stage

The **Expanding** organization shows a good sense of direction. Now, coordination is the key to success. Imminent success causes the key decision makers to focus on returns—profitability, efficiency, increasing member satisfaction, or growth in numbers.

The role of management in this stage is to bring all facets of the operation into balance, reinforcing the importance of standards, quality, and long-term success. Frequently, though, resource allocation is driven by personalities rather than a plan, and being able to guide the organization through this stage requires strong interpersonal skills. The potential for tremendous growth is clearly the carrot that motivates the expanding entity.

The computer industry is a good place to observe what transpires during the Expanding stage. The automaker Hyundai is involved as well with personal computers, and its foray into the high end and mass markets of the PC industry, with a new design and lower price than competitors, held a lot of promise. The key variable was the management expertise of Edward Thomas, who had proved his mastery at producing growth in organizations at this stage with a tremendous track record in mail-order computer sales. Thomas's ability to realign systems and processes enabled Hyundai to custom-build PCs and give extremely rapid turnaround for repairs.

The story of Comcast, a cable TV company, is much the same. Like other cables, Comcast made a bid to expand into the cellular telephone business. Although the gargantuan companies like Bell Atlantic virtually own the industry, Comcast, through the entrepreneurial energy of its top management, has targeted areas for significant growth. Telephones are used extensively for data transmission via computer modems, and Comcast saw this as an avenue to stretch its capabilities. Its plan relied on the ability to coordinate the efforts of the smaller businesses that it gobbled up and to execute an aggressive and creative plan.

The Maturity Stage

As much fun as the expansion is, at some point even the best organizations fall asleep at the wheel. The **Maturity** stage represents this inevitability. It isn't so much that the organization matures but that the external setting changes more rapidly than the organization's sensitivity to it, leaving everyone to play catch-up.

Most of us are familiar with United Way, whether from consenting to payroll deductions or volunteering at one of its member agencies. But after 100 years of growth, unparalleled success, and bright future prospects even in the face of a disrupted philanthropic environment, United Way may have focused more on what was happening inside the place than in the environment. Case in point: one of the early signs to United Way that important changes were taking place in customer preferences should have been the craving of the public for choice in where their funds actually went. People who were concerned about homelessness, let's say, wanted to make sure their bucks went to help the homeless. The "donor option" concept became a thorn in United Way's side because they were not ready to embrace it. This caused them to have to react to the customer rather than respond. Smaller charities used this opportunity to suggest that United Way spent a larger portion of each dollar just to fund their huge staff payroll and therefore were less efficient than their competitors.

The truth was that United Way's administrative costs were lower, in many cases, than its single-issue campaign competitors. If you think about it long enough you'll see that in concept, they have always had donor option but their structure had made it hard for them to see it that way and to shift their emphasis in line with the environment.

What you see in the maturing stage is akin to hardening of the arteries in a human body: great people, great product, and great system, but structurally the message never quite makes it through to the brain. In this stage of development, management style can become the make-it-or-break-it variable.

The Entrenched Stage

Just like a human being, as an organization gets older, it tends to get bigger, its reflexes get slower, and it can get set in its ways. Sometimes getting older can mean getting better, but the line that separates them can be fuzzy. At the **Entrenched** stage, the survivors of Maturity have to draw that line with clarity and accuracy. Suppose new management does come to the rescue and provide the proper perspective on the environment. How do you impart flexibility to that structure and continue to prosper? Management must have the courage to evaluate all activities in light of the mission and environmental conditions, and make changes accordingly. Personnel changes may also have to be made, as well as redefining the contribution of departments and functions.

In the world of accountancy, the term "Big Eight" was known to represent the eight largest firms. It's now the Big Six, for obvious reasons, and things are still changing. The accounting industry grew like gangbusters during the late 1970s and well into the 1980s, reviewing and approving the books of their clients and providing consulting support of various types. As Expanding organizations they grew, but as the environment began to change, they found themselves maturing. They became bogged down, top heavy, inflexible, and oblivious to what was happening outside and inside. The woes of the financial industry, especially the S&L dealmaking that was uncovered, landed many of the Big Six in court, with resulting settlements in the hundreds of millions of dollars. Also, as fewer companies are gobbling up others, revenue from client billings has dropped, and there is relatively less demand for accounting services overall.

Entrenched organizations can seize opportunities in the midst of this kind of maelstrom if managers are willing to do what has to be done. Enter Jon Madonna, CEO of Peat

Marwick, the smallest of the Big Six. Madonna possessed the courage to do the nearly unthinkable: he not only cut the partnership rolls of Peat Marwick, but like many of the accounting and management consulting firms, he implemented an "up-or-out" policy that forced professional staffers to develop broader capabilities. New systems were introduced, including a team approach to link traditional accounting with less orthodox consulting.

Those who manage organizations in the Entrenched stage must bank on their creativity in order to enable the organization to think differently about the operation. Only time will tell whether Madonna's approaches will produce long-term results, but his track record suggests that he will at least avoid moving blindly to the final identifiable stage of change.

The Complex Stage

In the **Complex** stage there is a major concern with how controls, checks and balances, and an almost oppressive hierarchy have created an inordinate amount or red tape and stagnation in the simplest procedures and systems. There is also a higher than normal quotient of employee apathy and cynicism, to the point that there is a cerebral consciousness in the environment that suggests that any attempts at improvement are futile.

Here is where managers who really understand empowerment can excel. They realize that employees are already empowered and simply need someone who will run interference for them and remove the obstacles to productivity. The concepts of team building, pooling of talents, and resources are vital, and those who can help people appreciate how their varying perspectives can actually blend to form a cohesive force can be near messiahs to an ailing bureaucracy.

Once people get to the not-caring stage, it may be too late, but I've learned never to underestimate the resiliency of the human spirit or the impact of a manager who knows how to tap into the fiber of that spirit.

An interesting example of change management at this stage can be seen in the recreation of Armor All Products, the company that became famous for its automobile vinyl-renewing polish formula. After years and years of growth in earnings, the company's creator and energetic founder, Alan Rypinski, sold the organization for a tidy sum and moved on. Over the following eight years, the company nosedived. It became stodgy, its systems became overloaded, and eventually it became incapable of changing directions in tune with a resegmented market.

Worse, the climate among employees had hit the skids, and there was little or no momentum available to turn things around. Then the company used an important principle: it went back to what it was that got it there in the first place. Management asked Rypinski to return to jump-start the business and bring some of his entrepreneurial zest to the vision for where they should be headed. In doing so, Armor All had lit a fire of innovation and commitment among the work force and is battling the plague of bureaucracy full force.

Managing Change: It's All in Your Mind

Russ Ayckoff, Kurt Lewin, and Mike Connors have been pioneers in developing tools to analyze change. They have given us a set of tools to help hone the use of instinct in dealing with change. The key is to distill that which is practical from an abundance of good theories. These tools also show us that the ability to steer people through change depends on having a well-ordered thought process to analyze critical situations, much the way Ken Blanchard has taught us to look at the situational nature of involving people in resolving issues.

As Figure 1-3 depicts, any issue that enters the organizational domain from smoking in the workplace to the implementation of merit pay—has the potential to create change. If you can discern whether change is in the latent, growing, peaking, or declining phase, it has critical ramifications for the way you deal with it.

The great American search for organizational change goes on, with most organizations failing because they expect one boilerplate approach, like TQM, to carry them through from A to Z. But change occurs in specific phases, and if you're going to carry it off, you've got to tackle each phase with an approach all its own.

Now there's **MASTERING THE CHALLENGES OF CHANGE**, the first book to address the Five Key Phases of Change—and how your company should navigate itself through each one. Here, in concrete, step-by-step terms, you'll learn how to ensure support and cooperation as your company wends its way through these stages:

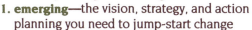

In the book, you'll master the Five Cycles of Organizational Change, with special goals, priorities and key issues for each.

1. **emerging**—the vision, strategy, and action planning you need to jump-start change
2. **expanding**—dismantling the culture of the machine—and supplanting it with a focus on quality, teamwork, and flexibility
3. **mature**—mastering the culture of the organization, removing blockages to doing business, and seizing the last chance to manage change
4. **entrenched**—strengthening weak spots, keeping communication open, and nurturing strong leaders now that change is in place
5. **complex**—the steps you must take to keep on changing, and stay fresh, before the "new wave" settles again into the "same old, same old"

Along the way, fascinating case studies of such major companies as IBM, Apple, Compaq, Lloyds of London, and McDonalds are included, to show how the Five Key Phases have been played out both for better and for worse.

Is your company ready for the five different "cycles of change"? Of course it is—with the A-to-Z blueprint for success you'll find in **MASTERING THE CHALLENGES OF CHANGE**.

About the Author

LEROY THOMPSON, JR. is president and CEO of Top Management Assistance, a management consulting firm to corporations and government agencies. He starred in the American Management Association's video production *Written Skills for Improved Communication*.

- **176 pages • 6" x 9"**
- **Published by Amacom in 1994 (60646)**

Publisher's Price $21.95

Member's Price $18.95

Earns one bonus credit toward the four required for your next Bonus Book

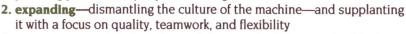

Change comes in phases. That's why your company's change
program needs a specific approach for every stage of the process.

MASTERING THE CHALLENGES OF CHANGE

STRATEGIES FOR EACH STAGE IN YOUR ORGANIZATION'S LIFE CYCLE

BY LEROY THOMPSON, JR.

Figure 1-3. Cycles of change.

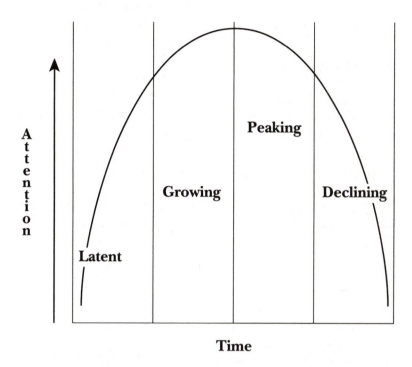

Managing Out of Cycle

Organizations typically attempt to deal with change out of cycle, that is, address it in, say, the peaking stage with actions appropriate for the growing stage. Dr. Ron Evans, when he was a management development specialist for the Commonwealth of Pennsylvania's 40,000-person Department of Public Welfare, told me once that "managing change" was the ultimate oxymoron. He recalled the time when the state's Corrections Department was concerned with the safety of guards in the event of a prison uprising and instituted a plan to train them in various self-defense tactics. If you know the state government procurement process, you know that it can't happen overnight. In fact, by the time the plan was released, proposals reviewed, a vendor selected, and the training completed, the threat of uprising had passed. A correct assessment of a situation is essential to getting better timing between the reality and the action we want to take.

Types of Change

Not only does change run its course in a cycle, but each change has a particular nature and degree of impact. Basically, there are three types of change:

1. *Transformational,* with an effect on the organization's overall direction. The Japanese computer companies seemed on the verge of doing to the U.S. computer companies what Nissan and Toyota did to Detroit. But as the other Pacific Rim countries, notably South Korea and Taiwan, expanded their capital markets, smaller U.S. companies got access to funds, and the supply of microchips enabled them to thwart the Japanese giants. Japan's entire focus, from laptops to mainframes, has had to undergo a transformational change in order to remain competitive.
2. *Methodological,* with an impact on how things are done—for example, joining the technology age.
3. *Tactical,* or midcourse corrections—for example, replacing one version of database software with another.

Different types of changes have varying impacts on an organization's effectiveness. Some changes have a direct bearing on the organization's purposes, while some have a greater impact on operating efficiency. Still other types are routine adjustments to systems and procedures.

Mastering the Skills to Manage Change

Managing change requires developing the thinking skills and mastering the analytical (as well as creative) tools. We will examine those tools and skills in the light of all levels of change, so you can see how to apply a commonsense thought process to real-world challenges.

Having a convenient way of adding some sequence and terminology to the task will not only help you to remember the major themes but will allow for the integration of major concepts in organizational change with principles of effective management. In the next few chapters we'll deal with the following concepts:

Strategizing:	The impact of vision and how to use it to create a climate in your organization that's rich with innovative thinking
Organizing:	The value of improving the processes and systems in the organization through which change can propel you to greater heights
Listening:	The role of feedback and interaction within the internal and external environment that will help you anticipate change rather than be its victim
Leading:	An easy-to-implement approach to getting people to want to do what it takes to move your organization toward its productive destiny
Recreating:	The ability to discern what options an organization has when it gets to the end of the road in the cycle of change

Preparing for Takeoff

No one model can say it all, mainly because even when done right, change of any kind brings with it its own special brand of resistance, so we'll touch on this critical piece of the puzzle too. That will bring definition and focus to the whole picture.

Now imagine us gliding down the runway, about to lift off to get a better view of what is happening here on the ground. Buckle up; here we go.

Two

The Concept
Of Culture

When you cease to make a contribution you begin to die.
Eleanor Roosevelt, American humanitarian and writer

Recently a lot of attention has been given to organizational culture, a concept with profound implications for all aspects of management, especially organizational change. Have you observed that in your own environment there are forces that seem to shape the way people see the organization and how they evaluate it as a "good" or "bad" place to work? These forces are largely intangible and often operate at a subconscious level, but their impact is obvious and pronounced. They dictate the nature of interactions between employees, between departments, and between levels of workers, managers, and executives, and they shape the nature of interpersonal communications, interactions, and attitudes toward the job. Most important, this concept of culture may be the key to understanding what it takes to address the management systems that grapple with the issues of a particular stage of change. Without an insight into the nature of these forces and how they influence the daily life of the organization, many well-conceived change efforts fail miserably, often leaving employees more jaded and cynical than they were before.

19

In every corner, we are on the verge of a major transformation in our concept of what management should be about and of what leadership should be composed of. Management and leadership are also central issues in this notion of culture because they relate to a set of expectations about how we should conduct ourselves and what we deem acceptable or unacceptable behavior.

What Exactly Is Culture?

If you consult your dictionary for the meaning of *culture*, you may not get much satisfaction. The technical rendering of the word relates to the "manners, customs, ways of thinking and behaving of a given group of people at a given point in time." Perhaps a better way to approach the meaning is to describe it more fully in ways that allow you to recognize the operation of these components in the real world of your organization.

Organizational culture works at different levels. On one level, it operates in the form of visible dimensions of behavior and conduct—elements that people new to the organization must learn in order to become accepted members. For example, typically there are norms for dress in the workplace. In many environments, not only are suits the standard but certain kinds of suits and certain color ties reflect the position and status of the wearer. Another example concerns policies and procedures that frame expected behaviors. In many organizations, it is taboo to leave before the boss does, regardless of whether you have completed the required tasks for the day. If you look closely, you will be able to observe any number of rites, rituals, or commonly accepted practices that are not only unique to the workplace but function as almost unspoken rules governing behavior.

There is also an invisible dimension of culture. Much of the management literature speaks to the importance of shared values and a congruent set of principles that guide employees' understanding of what the purpose of the organization is intended to be. In other words, an element of culture is that we unconsciously (and sometimes even consciously) expect people to believe the same things to be accepted as part of the group. These belief systems are usually imposed by top management as a means of forging consensus toward business goals and objectives. Beliefs about teamwork and being a team player, for example, become invisible yardsticks for gauging who is suitable for promotion.

Culture also encompasses the organization's views on change—usually a shared sense that few things will change. This concept is both a tremendous strength and a weakness. The strength is the organization's ability to perpetuate itself and reproduce the actions that make for continued success. In any business, profits come as a result of demonstrating consistency in the delivery of the product or service. The weakness is that when change is needed, convincing the culture that change is beneficial can be an enormously difficult task.

Culture conveys as well the ability to pass on the accumulated knowledge to new members. This is a mysterious process that takes place in subtle ways but essentially is a matter of people learning what works and educating others to duplicate it. This learning process is based on a propensity of the human mind to find and establish patterns of thought or action that seem to support the requirements for survival. In organizations, we learn to discard any behavior or way of thinking and believing that does not lend itself to the culture's concept of preserving itself. Here again, this is a mixed blessing. The benefit is that it enables a group of individuals to create norms that facilitate the operations of the organization. It is a major ingredient in achieving consensus. The downside is that when the pattern or norm becomes outdated, it will still be perpetuated. In the most serious of instances, the external environment no longer complements the organization's cultural norms, and the entity slowly and painfully becomes extinct.

It is important to be able to analyze the type of culture you are dealing with in order to understand the stage of change that you are in. The two go hand in hand. Various theories of change and culture suggest a powerful interaction between the two. The knowledge of how to manage that interaction is at the core of effectiveness in guiding the organization into the future. For example, the implementation of technology in an environment where the culture thrives on personal contact can create enough resistance to cause all the technology's advantages to be lost. More frequently, we see organizations whose cultures have minimized the value of employees try to implement quality improvement programs that rely on their involvement. These efforts also typically fail because the current culture is not conducive to them.

The Single-Culture Myth

Some theorists believe that the existence of a single culture in an organization can be pinpointed based on the presence of the sense of shared values. They see the function of culture as removing the inconsistencies in how people understand and interpret the visible and invisible dimensions of the organization. In the effort to promote this collective agreement, there is an intolerance toward any viewpoint with the potential for undermining this agreement. Employees are seen as rallying around the espoused direction and behavioral norms that have been promoted.

Perhaps this notion may have had some influence in earlier times, but in today's organizations, we see something altogether different. First, the consensus notion promoted by top management tends to lose its realism moving down the hierarchy. Employees are either too far removed from the perspective of top management or, worse, have become sufficiently jaded to the point that they do not believe there are any shared values. Second, the inconsistencies between what management says it wants from others and what it does splinter the way employees in different positions view the organization and how it responds to the environment.

Interviews conducted at a Fortune 500 manufacturing company revealed some interesting distinctions along this line. When operators at the working level discussed their perspective on the organization, they spoke of it as being a cut-throat, dog-eat-dog workplace where everyone was out for himself or herself. First-line supervisors revealed that they felt the workplace was one where their fate was at the whim of their bosses, and everything revolved around what management wanted. They saw the company as a place where they had to take care of their employees and make sure they had everything they needed to do the job. Finally, the executive group reflected their need to direct and govern what was happening at other levels, since it didn't appear to them that a critical mass of employees had enough personal commitment to the goals of the organization.

Another interesting slant in this same organization was to talk to employees in different functional areas. Those in the marketing department felt they were more or less the hub of the company. They tended to be a bit critical of other departments' lack of responsiveness. Those in the manufacturing department also considered themselves the center of attention and felt other departments had an unrealistic idea of what was possible. Employees in administration felt relegated to a position of inferiority in the company.

These insights suggest that there may be some serious flaws in the commonly accepted notion of a universal culture's existing throughout an organization. Rather, there may be several cultures present, determined by a complex set of variables. How people interpret the stated norms and promoted behaviors seems to differ significantly. The presence of these subcultures makes it difficult to generalize about where employees are in their perspective and attitude toward the organization and thus places a heavy premium on management techniques that encourage discussion, conversation, and sensing sessions to learn how the various components of the overall culture feel and how they relate to the whole.

Fundamental Cultural Factors

The culture of an organization has a large bearing on its success.

Customer Value

One clear cultural parameter in this regard is the attitude of the organization to its customers or those who use its services. I do not mean the stated dimension but what actually is done or not done on behalf of customers. Just about everyone talks a good game—"customer focused," "service oriented," "product quality," and so on—but organizations that follow through on these promises and deliver the value to customers will tend to prevail in the marketplace. The desire to serve and take care of customers must be part of the belief system of every employee. It must be built into the structures, procedures, and reward systems. It is also easy to see when these elements are lacking. Let's call this factor **customer value**.

Management Sensitivity

Another fundamental cultural attribute that can be observed is the attitude of management, especially in the executive ranks. In one health care organization, there is an unwritten rule that forbids lower-level employees from socializing with people in management ranks. This type of rule is indicative of a culture in which position and title perhaps have more importance than competence and contribution. There is also an interesting interplay between management attitude and taking care of customers. Frequently an organization is prone to treat employees and customers in the same way. In other words, if your management culture is not sensitive and humane in its approach to employees, you may see the same problems with respect to the way customers are treated. This is the **management sensitivity** factor.

Capacity for Change

Finally, any culture that does not accept that risk, change, and challenge are constant features of the environment will find it hard to achieve or maintain success. Organizations whose values focus more on stability of the status quo than on opening itself up to new ideas are typical of those who fail. Breaking traditions and abandoning familiar rituals is obviously not easy to do and, in fact, accounts for the power of culture in that it can forestall the precise adjustments that most people really embrace as necessary. The degree to which these factors are present will help you to evaluate your organization's particular cultural tendencies. This is the **capacity for change** factor.

Cultural Patterns

The relative presence or absence of the factors of customer value, management sensitivity, and capacity for change describes the basic cultural patterns that you'll see functioning in the real world. I have identified five basic patterns:

1. *Opportunistic:* There is a high concern for the needs of customers, management exhibits a strong sensitivity toward the needs of employees, and change is seen as a friend, not a foe. If you were to spend some time inside the Saturn automobile organization, you would feel the excitement and energy that this culture creates. It's important to realize that no culture will be perfect, the openness and freedom of this culture compensate for the stress and pressure of the business environment. The battles are many, but so are the rewards.

2. *Transitional:* Equal emphasis is placed on customers and change, but management sensitivity has waned. Often these organizations have enjoyed tremendous success but encounter the need to buckle down in order to streamline their operations. Insiders at Apple, Inc. might suggest that the competitive pressures in the computer business have begun to bring about some of these tendencies in their own culture. The workplace culture becomes more mechanistic and perhaps slightly less personal, but the trade-off may be worth it if efficiency increases.

3. *Transformational:* Customers are valued, management is in touch, but there is significant resistance to new ideas or new ways of operating. The degree to which this culture has

damaging results to the organization depends on the external environment more than anything else. If the environment is stable, the capacity for change has much less of a priority. As competition or other factors impinge on the organization, its culture will adapt until it extends itself fully. The current condition of fast food industry companies like Hardee's or Roy Rogers reflects this type of cultural pattern. They tend to follow their competitor's lead rather than pioneer new approaches to the business.

4. *Defensive:* A low value is placed on management sensitivity and only moderate attention on customers and change. Certainly an organization is a collection of subcultures and it would be unfair to suggest that this is a less rewarding environment to work in, but where you can see the visible manifestations of this pattern, employees will certainly feel that way. It is a place where people wander aimlessly, hoping for someone or something to provide direction. Sadly, the employees who are a part of the Kmart organization would reflect some of this sentiment depending on where they were located and at what functional level they were employed at.

5. *Hostile:* There is an overall lack of focus on customer value, management sensitivity, and capacity for change. There is not much organizationally encouraging or motivating in this setting. Many big-city school systems exhibit this cultural pattern, largely due to the pressure placed on them by a rapidly changing "customer," as well as from outdated modes of thinking and behaving. The tragedy of this pattern is that the pendulum swings towards rite and rituals and away from results and rewards—this in spite of the competence and dedication of many employees.

Making Culture Work for You

Sources of Cultural Strength

It's hard to judge whether an organization as a whole really has consensus on its cultural norms. We've already discussed the notion of subcultures in contrast to the notion of one unified expression of culture. A further consideration is to understand where the source of strength of the culture emanates from.

Most studies of organization behavior put a lot of emphasis on the role of an individual leader (such as the founder of the business), who establishes a set of norms and expected behaviors. If the organization does well, these norms quickly become part of the fabric of the workplace. People who become heroes are those whose performance, character, and personality reflect these qualities. Stories told in the cafeteria become legends over time, and through this process, the cultural patterns become part of the foundation of all future activities.

Even when new leadership evolves, these practices endure. If the internal and external environment continues to support the success of these practices, everything is fine. But if the environment is disrupted, the very factors that made for success now spell disaster. The norms that govern the workplace now become barriers to accomplishing the purposes of the organization. This view of the dominant role of leadership needs to be replaced by a more balanced approach.

Adaptability

The long-term success of any culture—whether a company or a country—has to be measured ultimately by how well it adjusts itself rather than on how strong it is. We all know that nothing lasts forever, but we seldom behave on the basis of that knowledge. Industries, competitors, product lives, and the like all have a cyclical nature, so it is a commonsense proposition to build adaptability into any profile for cultural preservation.

Leadership

Another issue regarding leadership is the reliance on personality to frame culture. One strong leader certainly can get things off to a fine start, but it takes a plurality to keep it going. The hierarchical disposition of the modern workplace may yet end up doing more harm than good. If the subculture concept really does represent the real world better than the belief in overall consensus, then organizations imperil themselves when they fail to create leadership at all levels. The traditions of restricting decision-making authority, access to information, and advanced notice of intended plans or programs must be jettisoned.

Individuals

Finally, this narrow view of leader-oriented culture reduces the emphasis that should be placed on each member of the group in formulating the culture. This may account for the presence of so many subcultures in a single organization. Without being given the chance to comment, evaluate, or provide input into what the rules should be, most employees seek out like-minded comrades and develop their own rules. It's almost as if after having been told they cannot play, they form a group of their own and play whatever other game they think will provide the emotional compensation for being left out. This has a destructive impact on the opportunity to generate any sort of consensus and reduces the culture to a process of putting on the right face regardless of what true feelings may be.

Prescriptions for Cultural Strength

Developing and maintaining an appropriate culture that has the capacity to adjust to change as well as motivating some degree of consensus is not quite as impossible as it seems. The prescription, in fact, is relatively straightforward.

Language

Throughout history, language has played a major role in defining culture. Groups are linked because they speak the same tongue or learn to speak the same tongue once they are grouped. Language in the organizational context refers not only to jargon peculiar to the business, but to the presence of a shared message about what the future should look like and what contribution the entity will make to that future. The presence of a common language is a simple but powerful element of cultural strength. If the owners of an organization's culture can get the people to speak the same thing, nothing will be impossible for them.

Membership

Membership in any group can be facilitated by a knowledge of the guidelines for belonging, as well as the criteria for expulsion or denial of membership. In other words, people need to know the rules. They also need to discuss, debate, and define them as a group in order to be able to live with them and to live by them.

Conflict Management

Every organization faces confusing, conflicting, and paradoxical circumstances in which there are no established rules. This is one of the strengths of the cultures in effective governmental organizations. Some employees complain that there are too many rules, and rightly so. The advantage, though, is that there aren't too many areas where some thought hasn't already been given to how a matter should be handled. When the situation occurs, there are already preexisting rules that dictate how to mediate and resolve discrepancies. Sometimes a culture's ability to manage conflicts in a prescribed fashion can help to prolong its life.

Sense of Hope

A culture's preservation is threatened when the members feel threatened as individuals. When a culture lacks the ability to come together and share its fears, it can't develop a collective strategy to counteract them. In this circumstance, everyone who bears the responsibility of leadership must add to the collective sense of hope, and each employee must have a role in making those hopes a reality.

Relationships

Sometimes achieving a particular end result is not as important as the process undertaken in trying to get there. The simple act of articulating how we should be treating each other, where we're falling short, and how we can get back on track can be vital to improving the quality of relationships. It also guards against deterioration of relationships due to hurt feelings and wounds. Employees will probably never be fully satisfied or happy with all of their interpersonal transactions, but the process of disclosure creates a state of health that is even better than happiness.

Rewards

One last element is clarity concerning rewards. It's important to know what they are, on what basis they will be given, and that consistency in both is ensured. A lot of organizations try to do this, most of them with mixed results. Many use money as the reward, believing it has enough universal influence; others try more complicated schemes. But few have the presence of mind to take a look at what the culture is already suggesting is valued by employees and work from that basis. Sometimes the culturally inspired rewards are not the right ones, but often they're just fine. The key is that if they are what people really place value on, they should not be ignored. Recognition from peers, commendations from customers, or opportunities for growth in current responsibilities are typical examples of these rewards.

The McKinsey Way

To see these principles in action, a good place to look is the internationally renowned general management consulting firm of McKinsey & Company, considered by many to be the top in its field, and for good reason. Since its founding in 1934, the firm has developed a reputation for providing analysis and recommendations to the world's most prestigious and influential organizations. It is by no means a perfect place to live and work, but its culture supports its intended purposes in an outstanding manner. It has also exhibited amazing capacity for change in a very tough business. How does its culture stack up to the prescriptions I have outlined?

Language

The major language that new associates learn to speak is based on problem solving—taking apart a complex situation, analyzing its components, and reordering them to function together better than before. The heavy premium placed on analytical ability creates a common bond in communicating with clients, fellow associates, and partners. It also creates a level of confidence in that ability that probably accounts for the firm's outstanding success.

McKinsey has become more or less the standard for consultancy of its kind because the business community has come to believe that if it can't solve the problem, no one else can. Once the firm is brought in on what is known as an engagement, a group of consultants quickly begin to come up with possible solutions and spend the rest of the engagement proving or disproving them. Their presentation to management is delivered in the straightforward idioms of "what the data suggest," "what the numbers say," and "what the following analysis reveals." The firm's language is practically bereft of opinion. What counts must be proved, or it doesn't count for much.

There are also dialects that derive from the problem-solving tongue. The firm's founder, Marvin Bower, used to indoctrinate associates with his treatise on the "will to manage" and how vital a role McKinsey professionals played in supporting the client's ability to take command of their situation.

Having a common language produces a sense of belonging, and in McKinsey's case it creates an air of uniqueness. Associates learn that they are the cream of the crop. Whether they really are or not is not the point. They believe that nothing is impossible, and so it seldom is.

Finally, this language permeates each individual's feeling about what kind of place McKinsey is to work for. Like any other company, it has its problems, but a prevailing sense in the culture is that so does everyone else, and therefore the things that many other workplaces bemoan McKinsey associates view as normal—just another problem to solve. Additionally, most of the consultants are constantly out of the office, which leaves little opportunity for office conflicts.

Membership

The most basic rule for continuing as part of this exclusive group is quite clear: continue to enrich and develop your skills—or leave. To outsiders that might seem harsh and almost Machiavellian, but it is very sane and humane approach to preserving a culture of this nature. This up-or-out policy is accepted by all as the standard. It applies as equally to partners and directors (a more advanced state of partnership) as it does to associates and senior associates (typically those who manage the daily operation of an engagement team). The job descriptions of these levels are quite different, but the criteria for success are parallel. This makes for relative clarity in performance evaluations and few disputes over who the most talented and sought-after team members are. There will always be some politics in any workplace, but they are at a minimum here.

Hand in hand with the "up-or-out" is the notion of putting the client first. This is more than lip service—it is a life-style. Experienced partners can be called in with little notice or preparation to deliver crucial presentations in front of a demanding board of directors. As with any successful culture its separate elements feed on each other and support the whole. The heroes are the people who know what key questions to ask to get the root of the client's problem and turn seemingly impassable barriers into major advances for the client organization.

Conflict Management

This is obviously the toughest thing for any culture to do elegantly, but it is done well at McKinsey. The diversity of ideas is encouraged; even the greenest of associates speak up. Being right is important but being a "thought leader" is a more valued quality.

Suppose that it is two days from the progress review when the key client executives will hear the preliminary findings of the McKinsey team and determine if more money should be spent on pursuing their insights. It is discovered that through an oversight by the client personnel assisting the team huge quantities of data missing. The team thought it had based its half-a-billion-dollar recommendations on 80 percent of the cost figures available; as it turns out the database used only captured 45 percent of that information! This means that they are about to tell the board of directors what to do with their company based on about 35 percent of their business. A real dilemma.

The newest associate on the engagement team, after first reminding the group that he "told them so" weeks earlier, suggests that a manual analysis from computer printouts could be done in thirty-six hours by two people working around the clock. Of course, he ends up being one of the two people, but his willingness to speak up saved the day and established the rules for an unprecedented situation.

One other aspect that helps deal with unforeseen possibilities is the almost slavish commitment to self-evaluation of the firm's impact on clients. Much like an internal auditing process, it forces everyone to look just a little bit ahead and try to anticipate what future difficulties might be. They do damage control long before there's any damage.

Sense of Hope

No organization can insulate itself from threats. Business is predatory by nature, and the best one can hope for is a position from which to sustain the attacks. McKinsey's culture has several components that satisfy this requirement.

The firm does exhaustive research on topics of interest among the world's leading organizations. The premium placed on analysis pays handsome dividends. It's almost as if McKinsey has become the repository of all there is to know about running the modern corporation. People like Tom Peters, Bob Waterman, and Kenichi Ohmae draw on the rich library of experiences and have published some of the most insightful works available. Their works reflect the thought leadership, depth of analysis and the touch of elitism that suggests that the answer, as well as the questions, come for the brain trust of the firm. When the business community digests these thoughts, they are certain of the facts that went into the formulation as well as of the practical value those thoughts will have in addressing their current and future concerns.

Another source of sustenance is the long-term nature of McKinsey's client relationships. Engagements can go on for years, and the firm prides itself on having served the same organizations repeatedly.

The culture thrives on the challenge of meeting the toughest problems of the most visible companies. The long-term relationship is made more solid by the fact that the firm has an outstanding reputation for maintaining confidentiality. McKinsey consultants themselves may stay tight-lipped with their own colleagues for fear of even innocently talking shop and releasing proprietary information.

The remaining source of security is the culture's emphasis on top management. Part elitism, part negotiating ploy, the fact is that it has meaning to clients. The firm will even turn down engagements that lack upper management focus or are deemed not to add value to a client's business. Any consulting organization that shuns work it doesn't believe in commands attention. In a way, it also reduces the fear factor within the firm itself. The attempt to be the best rallies people. It causes them to worry less about what badthings could happen and instead energizes them to try to make something good happen.

Relationships

If business is predatory, then consulting is cannibalistic. The culture thrives on competition, and the same people with whom you must demonstrate good team play are the same ones you are battling for the one partner spot that your office will probably fill when the firm's personnel committee meets. This dynamic breeds a very delicate climate where it would be easy and natural for the competition to interfere with the team play part of the job. There is no written policy here but a very definite cultural attribute that helps this situation: open acceptance of the fact that everyone is a bright person. The respect that this understanding breeds minimizes the need to challenge the capability of colleagues and also leads to courtesy and deference to others. Also, old hands know that the person they embarrass today may be their engagement manager in six months.

The absence of the typical office setting and the lack of any pronounced hierarchy provide a forum for managing interpersonal relationships. Anyone can talk to anyone else, and if a team member's behavior is getting in the way of meeting the client's needs, it can be addressed. Naturally, new people are more judicious in taking these liberties, but the up-or-out policy injects the culture with a degree of professional candor that is seldom seen elsewhere.

The lack of hierarchy also limits the potential for excessive concerns over career development. There is no regular supervisor to please or manager to figure out. Those who are recruited for the best engagements are chosen because they have demonstrated their value in their previous efforts. Personalities always have a role to play, but at McKinsey playing favorites in any extreme fashion is ultimately risky.

Finally, in this culture, big egos are a norm. In the typical workplace, employees tend to minimize the intrusion of their egos in order to become accepted by the group. At McKinsey, there is relatively little attention placed on displays of egotism. In fact, the culture subtly encourages the growth of ego in the sense that greater confidence in one's prowess usually benefits the client. There is so little benefit in discourteous displays of egotism that only the most insecure of consultants fall into that trap.

Rewards

This is one of the strong suits of the culture. At the basic level of incentive, the chance to move up in the firm is what appeals to people in the long run. The career path is organized to reward progressive evidence of expertise and new challenges at each level. For associates, the idea is just to survive the hours, the hotel food, and the time and expense reports. If that works out, reaching the level of senior associate provides a nice boost in an already handsome salary and the chance to manage engagements. It's no less work than other team members have, but the thrill of being the point-person is a big deal.

Somewhere in the six- to eight-year range of tenure, the chance to become a principal is based on identifying a new area where the firm can expand its capabilities. After a few years as a principal, the ability to bring in new clients can result in becoming a full partner and, with it, a nice block of shares in the firm.

This structure works well mainly because of the clear requirements and the division of responsibilities. Senior associates, for instance, have no pressure at all to bring in new business. The challenge of being a principal bears little resemblance to those faced by partners.

Another tremendous source of reward is actually fed by the up-or-out policy. Even those who leave still manage to go "up." It is very common for ex-McKinsey consultants to become CEOs of the firm's clients. After a couple of years of extensive study and presentations before the board of directors, the client surmises that the McKinsey consultant is the best one equipped to carry out the recommendations. The knowledge that no matter what happens during tenure with the firm, the odds are that you will land on your feet is a tremendous motivator.

Perhaps the most gut-level reward is the work itself. In the vast majority of cases, these consultants are making a difference. Even when they are not, it still feels as if they are, and that makes a real difference. There is an intimacy with business that comes from looking into the deepest parts of a client organization and figuring how to manage its affairs. For the types of individuals that the culture attracts, being a change agent and the guardian of their future potential is an awesome responsibility.

The McKinsey Mold

When you add these numerous attributes together, you end up with a culture whose strengths dilute the impact of its weaknesses. There is definitely a McKinsey mold, which means that the contributions of individuals who do not fit the mold are not valued. This creates an inbred quality to the culture, which may be an issue in the future, but to this point the concerns are minimal. The fact that the firm has a global presence pushes any serious threats further into the future. If anything, this fact alone may be an important insight into making culture work. McKinsey's problems always seem to be down the road, and McKinsey typically gets there ahead of them.

Creating Cultural Change

As long as things are going fine, as they are with McKinsey, culture is almost a nonissue. But what if things aren't going so well? When do you need to think about ways to change the organization's culture? How do you respond to the demands that the environment is placing or will place on your ability to succeed? The literature abounds with formulas for making such changes, and there is no shortage of theoretical premises for cultural change. But reality may tell a different story. The truth about changing an organization's culture may be that you can't, or it may take so long that the investment may not be worth it.

There are other obstacles as well. The subculture concept suggests that you'd never really know if the culture had really changed, there are just too many factors that interact with one another to provide any definite results. You can change the organization chart, realign departments, and institute new policies, but to what degree have mind-sets been altered? Usually not much at all, especially in the short run of three to five years. By that time the environment may well be prompting some other response, and so off you go again.

It's also nearly impossible to get consensus on the need to change the culture. Sure, there will be a clear recognition that something needs to be done, but the standard reaction will not be cultural change. It will be the need for more staff, less bureaucracy, newer equipment, more money, and the like, but not real change. When things aren't going well, it's likely that someone is actually benefiting from the confusion and may work hard to preserve the status quo. Even when preservation is not the goal, protecting one's position and avoiding blame for the unsatisfactory conditions may be strong motivators to resist examining the culture.

As we'll see, much of the basis for cultural change depends on where the entity is in the grand scheme of organizational change and the particular stage that the entity will undoubtedly travel through. Each of these stages presents its own obstacles and challenges. It may be that these obstacles and challenges dictate the type of culture you can expect to see develop as part of the natural process of change.

The Results-Oriented Approach

So what's a leader to do? The key may be in looking for ways to bring out the positive attributes of the current culture and strengthen its ability to produce results. The point is not to create some new culture but to recognize the inherent resilience of an established culture and to find ways to use that resilience to the organization's advantage. Is the organization's cultural pattern Opportunistic, Transitional, Transformational, Defensive, or Hostile? We know where the strengths and weaknesses lie with each pattern and can manipulate them to produce better results.

A Transformational culture in need of change would seek to add impetus to its focus on customers by strengthening its marketing approach. In the Defensive setting, new leadership can be raised up to embrace a new agenda and build on the capacity that exists in this setting. The Hostile culture is void of strengths, but in fact, it is nearly culture-less, in the sense that it is almost totally out of step, internally and externally. Such cultures are probably on the verge of extinction and may therefore present the only real opportunity for cultural change.

The benefits of a results orientation are several. Meeting the needs of customers, increasing management sensitivity, or rethinking the scope of products and services can become tangible goals. Each of these embraces systems, structures, policies, procedures, and the like and can also touch on the less visible elements of core values, basic beliefs, and relative levels of consensus. The latter group will always take longer to solidify, but having a clear target adds focus to them. In this way, leaders can trumpet the necessity of, say, putting the customer first while concomitantly making alterations in the functional operations that are needed to make this work. With this type of approach, employees in any particular subculture can be reached by championing specific accomplishments and the specific way they can contribute, as well enabling the identification of common denominators between subcultures.

Implementing a Results-Oriented Approach

In subsequent chapters, we will look closely at the skills and techniques needed to deal with organizational change on the grand scale. There are a few key ideas with respect to cultural issues that are useful, and a consistent theme is the priority given to the role of leadership at the very top of the organization. The sincerity of these people concerning the reinforcement of core values and their diligence in making alterations in functional operations are vital to cultural change.

Jack Smith, CEO at General Motors, has had to face the task of rejuvenating a bureaucratic climate that seems intent on self-extinction. On the invisible side of the culture equation, there is no apparent sense of direction or vision among the GM executive and managerial ranks. Inter- and intradepartmental communications are ineffective at best, and there is a tremendous void in the perception of the overall business strategies that are needed. On the visible side, the structure is so complex that even the most routine tasks take inordinate amounts of time. Decision-making processes attend more to the politics of avoiding controversy than in getting good products out to customers in a timely fashion. Most functions, from purchasing to production, operate as if they were in totally different organizations. Management as a whole is cut off from the workforce, physically as well as emotionally. The result is a culture that can't produce any results, with the choice often being not to ship any vehicles at all or send out low-quality ones. This culture is the hallmark of the Complex stage.

Jack Smith has made some inroads, based on his ability to develop clarity of purpose and convince key subcultures within the organization that improvement is possible. He has backed up his rhetoric with actions, consolidating departments, streamlining functions, and selling off losing operations. Without this type of leadership, the task of turning GM around would be impossible. Even more ludicrous would be trying to change a culture with a workforce of over 300,000 people.

Many efforts at organizational renewal put their emphasis on creating a new culture without understanding the one that is already there. This knowledge is required to get down to the basics of building on what's still standing and on fixing the things that are broken.

Three

The Dynamics Of Industry Change

Even if you're on the right track you'll get run over if you just sit there.

Will Rogers, American actor and humorist

The examination of culture provides the foundation for understanding and analyzing the internal factors surrounding organization change, and in subsequent chapters we will apply that foundation to specific situations. But it is also critical to appreciate the context within which these specific situations occur: the bigger picture of change within industries themselves.

These changes are imperceptible on the surface. No newspaper will report them; no business analyst will comment on them; even the most astute manager will not observe the signals that announce them. And quite often there are no signals—only aftershocks.

As a student of organizational change, you need to develop a framework to anticipate the areas and dimensions of the industry that you are part of, if only to give you some lead time to position your organization properly. Obviously an industry is just a conglomeration of suppliers, customers, and competitors whose interplay is affected by changes in their structural relationships. While we wouldn't refer to presence of a culture, there are predominant behaviors and strategic norms that most of the players within an industry exhibit. In fact, it is often impossible to escape the forces that these industry dynamics exert. Although not as definite as the analysis of specific stages of change, there are some clear criteria that will ultimately help you determine where your particular organization is in its own change process.

Factors Affecting the Cycles Of Industry Change

The power of the external environment is that it shapes options for the future within limits that many managers seldom pay enough attention to. But even the best organizations can be negatively affected. The key is not just having information but the ability to put the pieces together. The organizations that can figure out the puzzle will turn out to be the winners more often than not. Those that fail to develop this sensitivity will become the losers.

Most industry decision makers are normally aware of obvious external factors such as the impact of regulatory change, new product innovations, or the entrance of major new players. But this awareness is also tempered by inhibitors that blur their vision, and many of these inhibitors are unique to the stage of change that the organization is in. For example, Emerging industries tend to have a very short-term horizon and exist in an overall state of uncertainty. This awareness ought to aid in the sharpening of senses, but it tends to limit the field of vision to concerns like reducing costs, establishing rapport with first-time customers, and making sure the supplier network stays in place long enough for companies to enter the business, to thrive, and to grow.

An industry that has reached Maturity may have an entirely different set of concerns. Now the environment will likely stress the accommodating of customers in new ways to compensate for the fact that the growth in the industry is beginning to flatten out. New product innovation is a bit harder to come by, and the key to success revolves around keeping profitability at a high enough level in order to buy time to restructure the way business is done.

In an industry, no one is controlling these forces, but everyone is affected by them. True, a given organization can be in a different cycle of change from the rest of the industry. Typically, this organization is taking the kinds of actions that prolong its position; it tends to be the current market leader or at least the heir apparent. A good example is Southwest Airlines. While the airline industry is in a state of decay, it is thriving. Outside of the complex issues of routes, rate structures, and the like, the real reason is that Southwest is promoting a new way of doing business. For the most part, though, industry dynamics have an all-but-pervasive impact on everyone.

Customers

Let's start here, since this area is likely to be the most easily discerned. Whether you are a private-sector company or a government agency, the attributes of your products or services that create the most impact on customers will be the gateway for change.

In the private sector, any organization that can satisfy those attributes can generate demand for a different mix of products. Just because someone in the marketplace has made a bigger, faster, more versatile product does not signal change. What is significant is when bigger, faster, and more versatile is no longer an attribute that is desired by the customer. If the customer's demand changes to price and ease of use, any organization that can offer even a substitute product or service will make headway. *This shift in basic needs of the customer is a clear sign of significant change in the industry.*

The public sector is not dramatically different. The grass-roots needs of a constituency are typically not clear on the public policy level until the media begin to catch wind of them. Once the cause becomes newsworthy, elected officials and government managers are forced to adjust their perspectives in line with what seems to be a growing demand for action on the issue. Frequently multiple issues are being surfaced at any one time, and it becomes a guessing game as to where the locus of influence will rest. The issue of using animals for medical testing is a good example here. When it began as the cause of a few environmental groups, it was ignored; as it became interesting copy for the evening news, it demanded action.

Whether public or private, these movements have the potential for altering the basis on which business is being done. In the private setting, established channels of distribution may give rise to new ways of getting the product into the hands of those who want it. New groups of buyers may even begin to surface as advertising and promotional strategies are realigned. Gradually these movements force just about everyone to reevaluate their methods and often their approach to serving customers.

Another ripple effect is the consideration of how much growth is possible in the industry. The concept of market share governs the decision making of most companies that sell products. Obviously the fewer potential customers who are discerned, the more hastily the changes in customer needs will be seen and felt. Since there is an established relationship between market share and profitability, organizations can be hurt tremendously by not calculating the growth potential in the industry accurately.

Products

Along with shifts in the wants and needs of customers, products and services themselves undergo change. Often it is hard to separate the two. Changes in customer habit patterns can result from intentional modifications in product or service offerings; changes in customer needs can motivate changes in products or services. It is the latter that more often prove to be the undoing of organizations.

In industries characterized by technology, experimentation, and innovation, the change issues tend to be volatile. In the information processing business, for example, the introduction (or even just the announcement) of a breakthrough on Monday can literally put people out of business on Tuesday. These cataclysmic upheavals aren't universal, but the principle is important.

Subtle modifications in the application of technology are taking place all the time and can pose threats on a grand scale. The American coffee industry used to be a premier player worldwide, but through seemingly minor modifications in the roasting process, the strength of the American brew could no longer compete with the South American and European blends.

Closely tied to changes in customers is the competitive structure of an industry. Typically, the greater the barriers to competition are, the more stable the industry will tend to be. But when the barriers are eroded or when a competitor changes the rules of the game, the situation becomes more chaotic. In the home video market, the smaller outlets believed that the "product" was the cost of the rental and priced themselves on a daily basis. New entrants changed the rules by making the product the length of time movie buffs can hang on to the video without paying extra. These new competitors get more money up-front and spare the customer the hassle of having to remember to return the movie the next day.

Products also have a life of their own, and the span of it is affected by all the other factors combined. The amount of time that a product stays on the market before it is replaced by something new is a good measure of how change is occurring. The shortening of product life cycles normally signals the beginning of major change in an industry since this shortening cannot continue indefinitely. Knowing this, the perceptive organization will be prepared to respond to the new opportunities that are created. Major competitors may drop out, leaving new customers for those who are left. Other competitors may enter, which means that to stay in business, everyone else will have to pick out a base of customers and specialize in serving them.

Cost Structures

The downfall of many enterprises, private and public, is that management does not know how much things cost. There are a couple of basics that are essential to running an organization. The first is the concept of fixed and variable costs. Fixed costs are expenses that have to be covered no matter how much business you're doing—for example, salaries or lease payments on office space. The greater the proportion of fixed costs to total costs, the higher the breakeven point for the enterprise will be. Variable costs increase or decrease with the volume of business—for example, travel expense, raw materials, or supplies.

When the cost structure of an industry begins to change, this may be indicative of major rumblings to come. Fixed costs change only when the structure of the business changes or when the basic methods of operations are changed. For example, most manufacturing industries have heavy fixed costs. In the early 1980s, when the ratio of fixed costs began to decrease, we also saw changes in profitability and competitiveness. The underlying cause was the increase in the price of raw materials, which ultimately altered the management approach to production and the products themselves. When you begin to observe changes in the fixed-cost base of the industry, you can be sure that more drastic changes will be forthcoming.

Another cost-related force in industry change concerns technology, or the after-effect of technology. A major cost component for enterprises within an industry are wages or salaries. Automation and advances in production processes create an opportunity to lower the labor cost component of total costs as fewer people are needed to perform automated operational functions.

Technology can create a significant competitive issue in an industry because it changes the basis of doing business. An enterprise can reduce its costs and increase its production. If the trend to a more capital-intensive approach doesn't become evident, it may be too late to make adaptations in order to remain competitive.

Strategic Success Factors

In any industry, there are probably five to seven critical elements that any enterprise in it must master in order to succeed. For instance, in the training and development industry, any successful organization has to be able to (1) establish economies of scale in product development, (2) manage fixed costs very closely, (3) recruit and retain a multitalented sales and consulting staff, (4) develop long-term relationships with organizations that are leaders in their respective fields, (5) develop intelligence networks to know what needs their clients are allocating line item budget dollars to, and (6) publish in their area of expertise. If these criteria for success in the industry change, it is a lot like starting over because the rules of the game have been rewritten and the deck reshuffled. This is why only the most agile organizations can sustain significant industry change. The key point here is that as you move along the change continuum, this agility becomes more a question of good planning and anticipatory decision making rather than divine providence or being in the right place at the right time.

In some cases, even more fundamental restructuring can occur. In manufacturing, to be vertically integrated meant managing all phases of the process, from supplying raw materials to distributing the finished goods. When companies in an industry begin to lessen the degree of integration, it is a sure sign of radical shift. Another example is service industries. In banking, for example, customers traditionally received a bundle of services at a set price with no real knowledge as to the individual value of each service. The unbundling of those services was a direct result of a new way of doing business. It affected every organization in the industry.

Changes in government policies and regulations can also change the strategic success factors. Currently the pressure exerted by environmental groups is having an effect on a wide range of industries, including construction, food processing, transportation, consumer goods, manufacturing, fashion, and energy. Regulations make it easier or more difficult for existing firms in an industry, as well as raising or lowering the hurdles for new ones to enter.

A Case Study on Industry Change

The information processing industry is an excellent arena in which to observe these dynamics as well as in appreciating the impact of those changes on the organizations in it. Technology has probably been the single biggest contributor to change with industries across the board and may be responsible for speeding up the transition from one stage of change to another.

For years we have been told that the expanded use of computers would contribute untold benefits to nearly all aspects of organizational endeavor. Production managers were led to believe that the machines would improve productivity and plant output. Marketing managers began to increase their revenue projections with the promise that databases would bring them closer to their customers and help to influence their buying decisions. Business managers were excited about the prospects of controlling and reducing labor costs because technology would require fewer people to do the same or more work. Human resources managers dreamed of the days to come when workers could operate in self-managed teams using technology to guide their efforts rather than depend on the oppressive hierarchy of supervision. And even office managers perked up at the thought of advances in communications that would make their jobs easier and improve their effectiveness. Finally, the wait appears to be over as the dreams and promises are coming to pass. Perhaps the single biggest contributor to the realization of the anticipated benefits has been that computers themselves have become easier to use. The idea of interacting with a machine has always been somewhat foreboding; now, the user-friendly mode of modern equipment has substantially reduced the fear factor. The proof of the pudding is that even employees whose jobs were not originally thought of as having computer applications are seeing the results. We will first look at information technology generally and then the computer industry.

Impact of Information Technology

Production Efficiency

The use of information processing technology has a tremendous impact on improving production efficiency in manufacturing and service industries across the board. One of the key changes that financial industries are seeing is that timeliness is leverage in satisfying customers. Most of us previously just accepted that it would take a certain amount of time to do business with our mortgage banker, debt consolidation lender, or insurance agent. Now, technology has been able to decrease dramatically the amount of time required for almost any function, from processing an application, to activating a term policy, to letting you know that you can go ahead and order the furniture for the new deck you can now build. Thus, the amount of time that it takes to acquire, process, and finalize transactions has become a distinguishing feature in the buying decision. And as these capabilities have grown, so have expectations.

The real positive impact on organizations is on the bottom line. Better responsiveness has increased business volume and, subsequently, net income. Whether we are discussing data transmission capabilities, automated tellers, satellite communications, or creative customer service telephone answering systems, the gains are clear. Time really is money, and the ability to cut the time spent on a procedure can translate into significant dollars.

In manufacturing, the benefits of information technology are as pronounced though perhaps not as visible to customers. These industries have always had some version of state-of-the-art equipment and a competence level in the workforce higher than they were usually given credit for. It was the ways in which these resources were deployed that tended to get in the way of productivity. Computers have helped to improve existing methods and work processes dramatically. For example, they have served to decentralize work, which has created more autonomy for the workers themselves. Now, factory workers get involved in generating creative solutions to problems, as well as contributing to the efforts of other areas. Apparently this autonomy was the right prescription for what was ailing factory productivity; many organizations have abandoned their traditional ways of operating.

The use of simplified technology coupled with the ability to delegate greater authority to the plant floor has been the major catalyst behind improvements in work processes themselves. By streamlining procedures, costs are also reduced, and so the benefits are quickly compounded.

In industries like retailing, inventory accounts for a large portion of the total costs. Being able to manage those inventories better through satellite technology has been a major source of change. Whether it's a hardware store or a clothing outlet, management at headquarters can monitor inventory movements in each store through point-of-sale networks.

Customers

Increasing sales revenue is a direct function of the ability to locate potential customers who are most likely to become buyers. Being able to do this quickly, repeatedly, and inexpensively is where technology has paid off. Access to databases has proliferated dozens of ways to pinpoint, or target, a particular market. For example, it is known that people living in a certain zip code will tend to have the same levels of disposable income and even the same purchasing patterns. Computers can track down these prospective buyers with minimal effort and cost.

Marketing methods overall have become more sophisticated. The telephone is now a legitimate source of revenue with the advent of pay-per-call services. While the more notorious uses of 900 numbers and the like are most publicized, there are an increasing number of legitimate business applications. Quaker Oats pet food division, for example, uses a 900 number to network with pet owners and to generate leads for their new products. The caller receives valuable information on caring for their pets and is given an opportunity to order products or receive additional information from the company. We have all probably experienced a telemarketing telephone call, from another human being or from a computer. While there are mixed reactions to receiving one of these calls, some industries, such as philanthropy, are purely a numbers game; the more people who are contacted, the better the organization does, regardless of how the general public feels about the methodology.

Technology has also expanded the range of opportunities to sell to customers. Sales representatives armed with laptop computers are able to make instantaneous changes to an order, saving the customer time and possibly aggravation. Delivery personnel can verify orders, locations, and receivables without having to go through channels. Service representatives can check the availability of parts, supplies, or substitute products right on the spot. In this way, technology makes every employee a potential salesperson.

One of the more interesting adaptations that this aspect of technology has to offer is the effect on suppliers and vendors. The federal government is one of the biggest markets for businesses in just about every industry, and within the government the Department of Defense has historically been an important source of opportunity. Increasingly, organizations that want to continue to do business with the Defense Department must be compatible with its technology. The Defense Personnel Support Centers, contractors for an incredibly wide range of products and services, are now educating vendors on how to use technology to communicate with them in every facet of procurement. This trend is just beginning to gain momentum.

People

Ultimately it is the impact of people that will determine whether technology has lived up to its billing, and the results at this point are clearer than ever before. As the nature of work itself has started to change, we are able to observe these results. One is that computers are starting to outperform people in the sense that many of the tasks performed by humans are better done by machines. Another noteworthy effect on people has been the contribution of technology to altering the structures used to manage. Loosening of the hierarchy, job sharing, flextime, and the like have all been made possible to some degree by technology. One of the fastest-growing "industries" is home-based businesses. The fastest-growing job structure is employees working out of their homes. In either case, being connected to the office or to a client by a modem is almost as good as being there. In some professions, it's better than being there. The savings in benefits and other expenses incurred in carrying an employee is worth letting them work in their own homes part time.

Home-based entrepreneurs could not exist at all if it weren't for the declining costs of technology. The growing acceptance of home-based businesses has been accelerated by their ability to deliver what the customer wants. In fact, because of lower overhead, in many cases they can do the job for less without any decline in quality.

One of the more subtle impacts is the displacement of management, especially midlevel executives. A major function of their jobs has been handling data and information; the process of gathering, analyzing, and reporting has long been the differential in job classifications and pay scales. But now we discover that by delegating authority to the plant floor or through equipping sales and service people, the information management task is already done. This is definitely a new twist. We have always been promised that this would happen, but it was assumed that it would be the application of technologies like robotics, with blue-collar positions hanging in the balance.

Within the typical office, the effects are no less apparent. Here is where we can observe some of the ambiguous results of technology. E-mail has been hailed as a time saver and a productivity enhancer, and in many industries it has begun to take the place of human contact. Yet there are times when interaction and discussion are required and simply leaving a message doesn't get the job done. The lack of human interaction may have other drawbacks, including adding to the already depersonalized sense of purpose that many workers complain about. But on the other side of the coin is the tremendous value of resources like videoconferencing, which can assemble a global audience with ease at comparatively low expense. The opportunity to tap into the wealth of knowledge and expertise is a clear benefit. To be able to reach consensus among key decision makers in short order has ramifications beyond what we can evaluate right now. If you add the use of cellular telephones or fax machines to the mix, then it becomes apparent that the very nature of what we call "office" is undergoing an incredible metamorphosis.

In a bigger sense, the very nature of what we call work is also being recast. It is uncertain what skill levels will be needed to operate the available technology, but it's clear that we won't need as many people to do it. The concept of self-managing teams is no longer just a notion; in many industries, technology is helping to make it the norm. This means that the idea of supervisors is on the wane, no matter how slow we are in facing up to it. This may be the biggest and most dramatic shift in the people side of organizational life.

And what about paperwork? Will we ever get out from under the heap? The office of the future may well be able to overcome the inundation of paperwork but not quite yet. Significant advances in techniques like image processing and CD-ROMs make it more of a reality. Coupled with the fact that these methods save money in the long run, it's easy to see why there is so much interest.

These developments should deepen our appreciation of the pervasiveness of the information industry. and yet it may have only just begun. What are the forces within the industry that will determine the continuation and augmentation of all of these benefits? Let's take a look at the operation of the industry dynamics we've discussed.

The Computer Industry

Within the computer business, nearly all of these industry dynamics have been at work. Based on what we looked at in the previous pages, there have obviously been some dramatic changes in customers. The growing comfort with the whole concept of technology and the realization of what it has to offer have spawned a near craving for these capabilities among consumers. Rather than simply accepting what is available, customers overall are now demanding that technology be developed to meet their needs.

There have been changes in products as a result of these advances. Miniaturization and increased speed and simplicity are but a few of them. Some of the major organizations went bankrupt in this area while others secured near-monopoly positions as product life cycles shortened. Cost structures within the industry have changed as well. What is clear above all other things is that the basic rules that perhaps governed the business are also being transformed. Let's examine the interworkings of these dynamics and especially the implications for specific organizations in the industry.

Storms on the Horizon

As recently as five years ago, even the most astute observers of the computer industry would not have given the following forecast: "dark clouds of competition bringing storms on the horizon." They would have believed that competition would create breakthroughs and some firms would come and go, but to sense the rewriting of basic rules that governed the industry was yet another thing. By and large this is what is taking place.

Some of the early warning signals should have been the announcement of staff reductions by several of the larger companies. But in this era of corporate downsizing and realignment of organizational structures, the signal was not picked up. When a company like Wang had to seek bankruptcy protection from the courts under Chapter 11 because it was unable to meets its financial obligations, more signals were given. Wang's problems went beyond product development or target marketing; they were the first contractions of an industry giving birth to a new way of looking at itself.

Although it's less precise to describe an entire industry in a specific change cycle, it's hard to resist the temptation, especially because it may have some validity. This tends to be the case for the computer business. At the time the warning signals were beginning to surface, the industry seemed to be on the cusp of the Maturity stage. This analysis hinges on how we interpret the emphasis placed on marketing by the major players, but I believe there are enough data to support it. In fact, the problems that Wang faced were evident on an international level as well, as firms in Italy, Germany, and France began to falter.

The major companies in particular found themselves in an environment that inhibited their ability to be experts in all phases of the technology business. Now they would have to choose a preferred territory, yielding potential opportunity for growth and spending their time perfecting the skills to do well in it rather than be successful all over the place. One of the warning signals occurred as far back as 1981 when IBM chose to offer the Intel microchip (the fingernail-sized device that makes a computer "compute") along with a standard Microsoft operating system (the set of instructions that tells the computer what sort of computing to do and how to go about it).

This was a warning of a new priority on marketing. Until then, companies in the industry led customers toward the purchase of systems that they thought the customer could make the best use of. The shift was now toward the customer's being in the driver's seat. This is the stage when marketing must become a conscious process; it thus represents the beginning of the Maturity stage in the cycle of change. What was to follow was a scramble of sorts where competitors were looking for that special place (and even places) of opportunity for growth.

New World Marketing

In the past, the area for opportunity was the manufacture and distribution of huge mainframe systems. This had been the mainstay of the industry and the hallmark of companies like IBM. But although the technology was there, the profit potential was not, as the growth of smaller, powerful personal computers became desirable and demanded by the market. The impact of the new thrust in marketing had to do with more than just advertising and sales promotions; it was part of a fundamental restructuring in the industry. Historically computer companies were as vertically integrated as the average steel company. The new requirements fashioned them more like a local boutique—still managing an array of offerings but all targeted at one type of customer rather than to everyone, as a department store might try to do.

This change in success factors and the advent of the Maturity stage present special problems to an industry that places an inordinate amount of pressure on organizations to launch new-product ventures in order to satisfy the demand of their customers or to develop new ones. The skill that most organizations learn in the Expanding stage do lend themselves to new product development, but often they're best at making what they have work better, faster, or for a longer period of time. Being innovative is more difficult than it seems even for companies with tremendous industry prowess.

In the technology business, the rapid pace of development and short product life cycles accentuate an already difficult task. This cycle wouldn't be treacherous if an organization would simply remember what worked in the Expanding stage and transpose it. To avoid the pitfalls of new product ventures, computer companies must do more than react on the basis of their own good ideas; they need to involve customers in figuring out what the product should look like and what it should be able to do. This is a skill that the Expanding stage teaches. Another critical skill is to make sure the various organizational components are involved in this process. The fiefdoms that normally accompany the design, development, and manufacturing process are deadly at this point.

There is no time for turf battles. You only get one shot to do it right and beat the competition to the punch.

The precariousness of finding this niche with the pressure on and without a grasp of industry cycles illustrates the effect of these upheavals. In an effort to accomplish the needed diversification, some organizations try to enter new areas without understanding that they may be entering a new industry. It also may be in a different stage of change than the one that their primary expertise is in. Many computer companies that had specialized in hardware have tried to find a home in the software field. This market has been dominated for years by the formidable Microsoft, with other enterprises showing real promise for capturing a dominant share of the business.

Software as an industry still shows many of the characteristics of the Emerging stage, where the design of strategy and being able to surprise the market are critical skills. This may explain why companies like Apple and IBM probably will not succeed as quickly (if at all) in their ventures to develop software such as operating systems and why the "Microsofts" will likely still be preferred even if their new stuff hits the market later. They are used to the process and do a good job of keeping their organizations in line with the inertia of the Emerging environment. But the concept of unbundling the vertically integrated nature of the computer business has been perceived as the new key factor for success.

The Trickle-Down Effect on Structure and Culture

The real implications of this sort of industry change for an organization are less perceptible than even the need for new product innovation. In the computer industry, the fact that customers know what is available to them will ultimately put pressure on the competitive culture to change in tandem. Ultimately, the net effect is to create momentum for change in the culture of the organizations that compete. The cycle is drawn in Figure 3-1.

In the computer business now, the only way to attract new customers is to offer more for less (a concept that has a counterintuitive ring to it). With more microprocessor power

Figure 3-1. Cycle of industrial/organizational change.

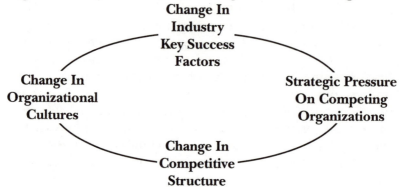

available to all competitors, innovation, advancement, and new product technology became the new industry standard. At the same time, the industry's falling prices and slim profit margins become the unavoidable norm. So for most competitors, business as usual means not making any money. Even the big machines, the mainframe variety, experienced the same behavior of rising capabilities but falling prices. Clearly, this has now become a feature of the cost structure and not an aberration caused by the popularity of PCs, as some analysts suggested.

From the customer's standpoint, the pressure placed on competitive firms is a boon. Customers can shop around, looking at a wide range of products, and put together their own system. The market dispersion and subsequent unbundling of technology offer consumers the chance to combine one company's machine with another's peripherals (printers, scanners, modems) and use yet another's software version. This new consumer role signals the dawn of new competitive structures.

For the major companies it appears to be a very concrete alteration of structures. Unisys, for example, essentially divested itself of its production capability as well as 45 percent of its workforce. Now it concentrates solely on distributing systems put together by other companies by developing consulting-type knowledge of the information processing needs of other industry clients. Other computer companies have set up independent operations and near-subsidiaries in order to do new business. Still others simply recognized that through decentralizing their operations, they could give business units the autonomy to pursue markets as if they were independent entities.

Overall, the basic structural game plan for an industry now in the Maturity stage revolves around some concept of marketing for new opportunities, conjuring up images of claim-stakers panning for gold on the western frontier. The version of this image for companies in the computer industry has them staking claims in particular product areas. One decides to go after high-baud modems (for transmitting lots of data over the telephone lines); another tries to corner the market on disk drives (the device you usually put a disk into with the information you want to compute with); another seeks expertise in system integration (helping a customer put the whole ball of wax together). At the same time, others abandon the hard stuff all together and sell customers the professional services to manage what the computers produce.

The common theme among all of these approaches is that they ultimately will produce significant changes in the culture of the organizations. Creating independent subsidiaries and giving profit-and-loss responsibility to previously centralized business units requires a different culture from the one they were grafted from. Short term, their success will definitely be more a question of marketing savvy or the lack of it. Over the long haul, though, the key will be how well they can develop the type of culture required. Many of these organizations are moving from an Opportunistic culture into a Transformational one without even knowing it. Unless they have individuals who are evaluating the organizational impacts of these marketing moves, much of that change will be taking place without their knowing that it's happening to them. Most managers within these organizations will be able to tell what the effect will be on the types of technological advancements that are possible in the future and even the rate at which new ideas can be spawned over the long term, but not enough will be looking at the cultural implications.

Company Profiles

IBM

For some time now, Big Blue has been blue, rocking and reeling from a series of bouts of amnesia—forgetting who they are and what business they are in. IBM is a good example of how an organization's own success can be its undoing. It's almost as if its ability to prolong its success in the Expanding phase created a culture that could not be unraveled. The focus on internal processes in many ways became a disease at IBM and now will likely provide the greatest inhibition to adjusting to a new industry environment. I don't believe IBM's problem is a lack of competence or creativity but a culture that can't make the most of either one.

IBM has determined that giving autonomy to business units and unbundling their products and services is the only way it can remain competitive and stay sensitive to the needs of customers. The question is how long it will last and what real prospects it has. In its Expanding stage heyday, IBM developed a reputation among its customers for having the solutions to their problems and the service to back it up. Now it will attempt to compete in a variety of markets, including the low end of the PC business, which it has recently entered.

One of IBM's biggest mistakes was marketing two versions of the Personal System, when it missed the PC opportunity. Its market penetration was much lower than projected as competitive products were in greater demand. That particular faux pas contributed to a precipitous decline in net income and the price per share of the company's common stock. Yet IBM still believes it can do well by selling less expensive systems. The problem will be that this is not what IBM is known for—not by their customers (who depend on IBM's technology) and not by IBM employees who have long prided themselves on technological superiority. You can change the structure, but you can't change the people or the mind-sets that they value.

Analyzing industry change and corporate culture should provide some keys to understanding situations like this. What would make the most sense for a company with an Opportunistic culture entering into the Maturity stage of industry change? There are no real formulas but taking into account what I've already noted about IBM, a few things seem to come to the surface:

1. Rather than break the company up into autonomous operating units, it would be more consistent to find ways to market what IBM has always done best and what is still needed and valued by its customers. IBM has always had a broad perspective on the field of information technology and would probably be better off finding new ways to make money using that perspective. The company already has a number of spin-off operations that have a track record in not just simply giving customers what they want but in staying ahead of them. This ability could be augmented by acquiring a better reputation for expertise within targeted industries, much like Unisys but with a lot more depth and scope of capability.

2. If the culture and bureaucracy is the inhibitor, then structural changes aimed at compensating for those inhibitions would be a smart move. Creating teams that cut across the departmental fiefdoms and promoting more sharing of information across those lines are appropriate steps to take.

3. There must be an effort to reduce costs in order to align operations with new industry norms. This would allow the organization to act more responsibly in relation to the dynamics of industry change and its own cultural parameters.

Apple Computer

Apple has maintained one of the highest profit margins among the major computer companies, and so the news of its deteriorating earnings and falling stock price is cause for concern. To remain competitive Apple has had to lower its product prices. This strategy has increased the number of units sold, but it means that Apple simply does not make as much on each unit as it used to. Other cost-cutting measures have been reactionary, such as proposed lay-off, facilities closings, and the like. Other shake-ups, even at the top of the hierarchy, are possible when an organization fails to examine the fundamentals of doing business in a new way.

Apple has always had a much smaller share of the computer market but has enjoyed a larger-than-life reputation for its technological insight. When other computer manufacturers were reacting to customers' fears of technology, Apple chose to build its operating systems in a way that encouraged competence by even the most reticent user. Instead of having to learn an intricate (and foreboding) system of commands, the Macintosh brand uses pictures on the screen (icons) that are activated by simply pointing and clicking. This technology attracted lots of customers who may have been putoff in the past by user-unfriendly machines.

The edge produced by the easy-to-use Macs didn't last long. Companies like Microsoft came up with similar versions of the Apple approach, such as Windows. This IBM-compatible operating system has the same icon-driven menus as Apple that make machines much friendlier. In addition, Apple has also made some forays into the "unbundling" abyss, trying to sell its operating system technology as a separate product. At the same time, the number and type of Apple machines available has congested the market for its products and presented an unclear image as to what Apple is really about as a company.

Sound familiar? Of course. It's quite similar to the moves made by IBM, just on a different scale and in a slightly different corner of the computer universe. Here again a company has failed to respond accurately to industry change, and its culture has gotten in the way. Much of the new-product emphasis for Apple revolves around using a slightly more enhanced microchip. But customers may not care about, say, having a 25-megahertz or 33-megahertz machine, especially since the speed of their use will also be influenced by the particular kind of software package they're running.

Again, as is typical for an Expanding stage mentality, Apple is trying to make the same stuff better as opposed to looking at customers in new ways. By focusing on aspects of the technology that only a few people understand, Apple is likely to cannibalize its business—that is, sell a new computer to someone who already owns an old one rather than attracting new customers. Apple's special brand of expertise, though, is in making the seemingly unfriendly aspects of computing familiar and fun. That's a more certain foundation to build on than trying to convince people that they really care about the underlying technology used in the machine itself. Perhaps looking for new ways to duplicate this expertise in products or services is a key to the future.

Compaq

Let's cap off this analysis by looking at what could amount to a success story. It also is a case of an organization that read industry change more accurately and accommodated its culture rather than tried to change or ignore it. Whether this is a conscious or unconscious act is not as important as the fact that Compaq is doing it. While the name may not be as widely known as the others, the track record is increasingly more impressive. During the late 1980s, Compaq began to go through the same industry and culture crisis but made some different decisions about how to respond.

After going through the kneejerk reactions of layoffs and cost cutting, Compaq began to ask the types of questions helpful to organizations whose industires are in the transition to Maturity: What is it that PC customers what from us? What can we deliver? The answers to those questions led to a strategy based not on technology but on price. Compaq has directed its competitive moves against other companies that sell based on price sensitivity and tried to create an awareness of the advantages of its product line.

An important point here is that in no way is Compaq abandoning improvements in technology. It's just that the main emphasis is not in selling technology but in using it to improve its ability to meet the market's demands and preferences. One of the latest innovations is the small, hand-held computer known as the personal digital assistant (PDA). Still in its infancy, it represents a potential source of growth that is worth pursuing. Compaq has also made some serious gestures toward the server market (computers or devices that link a number of other computers together in a system). The competitive approach is the same in all instances: to present the user with a lower-priced or cost-saving alternative to the other folks.

The final point about Compaq is to recognize the change in culture that had to be accomplished in order to take advantage of the opportunities created by industry change. As with all of the others, bureaucracy was threatening to smother the genius and resilience of Compaq's employees, but management had the courage to make change at the top, where it is usually needed most. It fundamentally restructured how departments and work units communicated with each other and with the outside world. This has enabled it to accent the qualities of a Transformational culture in line with the requirements of an industry in Maturity.

Each stage presents a unique set of properties and implications for culture, as we have seen in these cases. A more thorough knowledge of those properties will equip you to understand where your own organization is—and perhaps where it needs to be.

Four

Strategizing in The Emerging Stage: The Culture of War

> Where there is no vision, the people perish.
> *Proverbs 29:18*

Within the context of this quotation lies the significant difference between organizations that are successful in managing change and those that are less so. The concepts of strategy and strategic planning have been badly abused, reduced to the status of a few grandiose statements of organizational intent or a looseleaf binder full of actionless goals and objectives. The word *strategy* itself is a military term and describes an approach to fighting a battle, and, in fact, the culture of the Emerging organization is best characterized as that of a war.

Imagine yourself as the commanding officer with two options: you can rush in to engage the enemy in hand-to-hand combat *or* sometime prior to the actual conflict, you can locate a hill overlooking the battlefield and figure out the best plan of attack. Competent generals would obviously use the second option. They would assess the strengths and weaknesses of the enemy relative to their own capabilities and monitor the movement of their troops in the critical routes in and out of the theater of operations.

The analogy should be obvious by now, and the process for applying this concept to organizations can be equally straightforward. An organization in any phase of growth will have a need for some degree of strategic thinking and planning. There are issues faced in the Emerging stage, such as the trade-offs between establishing long-term direction and seizing immediate opportunities, that make the idea especially valuable. In fact, the ability to balance opposing needs of the organization is one of the principal reasons that strategic thinking is a vital tool.

The Stuff That Vision Is Made Of

Providing a Framework for Decision Making

Emerging-stage organizations often find themselves in need of a compelling vision for their future that will give them a fix on their direction and serve as a framework for making decisions today. An organization's future direction is essentially the sum total of its daily decisions. When this framework is absent, daily effectiveness and long-term viability are hurt. When executives, managers, supervisors, and line workers have no knowledge of where the organization is headed, they have trouble evaluating whether a particular course of action fits into the likely scheme of things. The result is that they will be paralyzed in their ability to act or, worse, their cumulative actions will take the organization in all sorts of directions.

In the Emerging stage, there is a window of opportunity—a time period of undetermined length when stability and opportunity can be successfully seized. Being able to implement the right decisions within this window is the key to managing change successfully.

Reinforcing the Sense of Purpose

Even the best strategic decisions lose much of their potency when they are implemented. If those who are affected are not inspired with a deep sense of commitment to these decisions, it will be difficult for the organization in the Emerging stage to make progress. In fact, employees in any setting have a fundamental need to understand where they're headed and what to expect to find when they get there. The analogy of a military conflict is also helpful in understanding the needs of the troops engaged in fighting this war.

The plight of the colonial soldiers at Valley Forge during the Revolutionary War paints a vivid picture of the Emerging organization. When the harshness of the winter had set in, these soldiers found themselves low on food and supplies, wounded, without shoes or blankets, and facing impossible odds. There must have been something very special about their vision of freedom and the sense of purpose that they shared; it not only gave them the will to survive but the strength to conquer. The only encouragement their leader, General George Washington, could give them was a rallying cry and a call to vigilance. Though they were mere words, the troops found in them heat, sustenance, and healing.

In the midst of change, managers are called upon to do nearly the same. They must be able to describe the benefits and rationale of their strategies with enough precision that employees are willing to make an emotional investment in the organization's future. Without that compelling sense of purpose, top management fools itself into thinking that compliance will be enough to produce results. If there isn't the hope of brighter tomorrows, the Delaware will never be crossed.

Defining the Role of Top Management

Painting a vision for the future is the job of top management. It is impossible to delegate, unwise to abdicate, and dangerous to ignore. Too often, though, leaders lose their balance and end up doing one of them anyway. Top management must make their concept of where they're headed known to everyone and continue to reinforce it. They must give clear guidelines as to what is expected from the troops and be willing to support risk taking and innovation. Top managers often say they advocate an organizational climate in which employees can speak their minds and their suggestions are given heed, but often managerial behavior creates a patriarchal climate instead, with maintaining the status quo more important than innovation.

For the Emerging stage to be mastered, top management must also ensure that strategizing is a continuous process, not an intermittent one. Planning retreats are a common technique used to get leadership focused on concerns of future direction. By removing themselves from the normal routine and taking the time to consider issues and information, managers are capable at arriving at a point of consensus on goals and objectives. The problem occurs when this gathering is seen as completed work and not the beginning of an ongoing effort. In addition, the job of communicating and reinforcing direction is never a one-shot process.

We'll look at the how-to's of accomplishing all of this by focusing initially on what can go wrong and what not to do.

Three Sad Stories of Failed Enterprise

Whoever said that hindsight was "20-20" knew what he or she was talking about. The following examples are in no way intended to point the finger of criticism at these organizations. They are merely instructional and point up some key issues. Also, these examples point to a snapshot in time and say little about the future viability of the enterprise. For some, failure can be temporary, and for others it's more permanent. Yet they are still sad stories, for behind the numbers and percentages are human beings whose lives were disrupted by change.

Lloyds of London: The Premium of Prosperity

There are few other corporate names that evoke such immediate and prestigious recognition as this 300-year-old insurance firm. Recent events have not only tarnished the name, but jeopardized the future of this venerable institution. With a history that long, it's hard to picture it in the Emerging stage—but remember that business cycles and industry conditions, not the organization's age, primarily determine what stage of change it is in. The insurance business goes through cycles as well as encountering periodic restructuring due to regulatory changes. Lloyds's strategy has been to attract wealthy investors who will underwrite their clients' policies. The typical approach for the majority of insurers is to carry forward the shareholder's equity from year to year. Lloyds's backers put up new money each year; they can enjoy the high returns when things are good or place their funds elsewhere when times are bad.

During the 1970s and early 1980s Lloyds's fortunes boomed as the strategy paid handsome dividends. But toward the end of the 1980s, a rash of claims related to natural disasters, oil spills, and decades-old liability suits bombarded Lloyds's bottom-line performance. The growth that Lloyds had experienced had now led to some of the typical difficulties faced by organizations when they are in this stage. For one, the company's own operating procedures lacked consistency, and as the financial experts put it, "sloppy oversight and careless underwriting standards led to an overexpansion of capacity." In short, Lloyd's now began to look for new approaches that would become particularly vulnerable to any catastrophic occurrences, which would call for large payouts on policies. It would look to corporate capital, rather than soliciting primarily from individual investors; and the implementation of a peer review process would reduce the problems created by sloppy underwriting.

Lloyds swooped in on the opportunities present in the marketplace. But common to the Emerging stage, those businesses grew without clear direction and continuity. One of Lloyds's traditional advantages over the competition was its lower cost base, but in the effort to reward executive performance, the company's salaries went off the scale, nearly doubling its fixed expenses as a percentage of total costs. The loose arrangement of Lloyds syndicates, brokers, and agents presented flexibility to seize opportunities but also posed potential vulnerability to change.

Surely we cannot criticize Lloyds's management for the events that created difficulties in the late 1980s—Hurricane Hugo, the San Francisco earthquake, and renewed enthusiasm for asbestos and pollution liability cases. (The fact that their competitors were hit even harder by these events will probably mean that the company will weather the storm.) The point is simply that greater clarity in direction and a focus on having a strategy for the future that dictates how the operation is structured can improve the organization's ability to anticipate change or to minimize the impact of that which could not be anticipated.

The Airline Industry: A Quagmire of Competition

The sad story to be told here is not so much about a particular company but an entire industry. The ups and downs of the U.S. airline industry are old news to most of us. During the 1980s, most companies incurred heavy debt burdens as they added new planes and new employees to expand their capacity in a robust economy. But as the economy weakened, companies began to falter, to fail, or to seek relief in Chapter 11 bankruptcy courts. In 1990 and 1991, the combined losses were in excess of $6 billion; in 1992, only one major carrier was expected to show a profit from its operations.

Since then it has literally become a war, with the emergence of new competitors, new route structures, international alliances, and cutthroat pricing schemes. One of the most feared opponents in this battle is American Airlines, which seems bent out driving out competitors (presumably in the name of eliminating surplus capacity) by saturating selected routes and employing guerrilla pricing. The company also uses a range of creative tactics, such as super-saver fares, frequent flier programs, and the like, which even have foreign competitors looking over their shoulders.

When a weak economy forces an entire industry into the

Emerging stage, pricing can be a major strategic weapon. In the airline business, this has become a vicious struggle, resulting in the elimination of competitors rather than the strengthening of the industry. Indeed, there has always been an absence of an overall strategy or guidelines for what would benefit the industry. Therefore, jungle warfare in the form of competitive pricing is the norm.

The warfare begins when a smaller airline becomes threatened by the infringement of one of the major airlines that needs the smaller one's routes to maintain its own profitability. Since the smaller airlines have fewer planes and fewer frills to attract customers, they lower their fares. The majors counter by matching the lower fares, and on and on and on. The net result is that fares are driven so low that no one can make enough money to stay in business. Bankruptcy will undoubtedly become the norm for small and large airlines alike until the health of the entire industry is imperiled. The real problem is competition and the importance in the Emerging phase of dealing effectively with it.

Overshooting at the Ritz-Carlton

The name itself implies luxury, and the purchase of that name in 1983 charted a brand-new course for the hotel chain. Its aggressive building of new properties in the Ritz tradition was in keeping with a resurgence of the entire hospitality industry. But no business environment is ever stable enough to put all eggs in one proverbial basket, and Ritz's failure to incorporate greater sensitivity to that environment may cost it its future.

In the early 1990s, most hoteliers began to scale back their operations. The Ritz-Carlton moved to increase theirs, entering nearly twenty new markets worldwide. The debt burden of these additions would have been manageable if occupancy rates had held up, but the recession, coupled with a glut of hotel space on a worldwide basis, put a severe crimp in revenues. Even given its high room rates, occupancy levels don't appear to be able to sustain the company's growth, leaving the Ritz on the brink of being unable to meet its repayment commitments to the host of lenders that financed the chain's initial spurt.

As an army prepares for battle, it must obtain adequate information about the movements of opposing troops and carefully survey the terrain, weather, and other conditions that could affect its ability to defeat the opposition. In the Emerging stage in particular, the first few encounters will likely determine whether an organization will sustain itself and progress through the other stages successfully. It must make calculated guesses as to the likely moves of its competitors and anticipate the direction and magnitude of various trends in customer behavior. Having a working knowledge of tools like strategic planning becomes essential to short-term viability and longer-term growth.

Strategic Thinking

Over two thousand years ago, Sun Tzu, the famed Japanese general, wrote *The Art of War*. In it he said that "the one who figures on victory at headquarters before even doing battle is the one who has the most strategic factors on his side. The one with many strategic factors in his favor wins and the one with the least strategic factors loses. Observing the matter in this way one can know who will win and who will lose."[1] Strategic planning offers a systematic way of "knowing" and building into the organization the resiliency to sustain the battles of the Emerging stage. The idea can get complex, but it really is simple. It is a commonsense approach to dealing with the uncertainties of change and is applicable to some degree in all stages of change.

Experts in the field typically offer a cookbook methodology consisting of a certain number of steps. There is validity to any of these methods, but their effect is often to obscure the importance of the process of planning in favor of the product

1. Thomas Cleary, trans. (London: Shambhala Pubs., 1991), pp. 9–10.

itself. In other words what the Emerging stage requires most of all is an organizational culture that thinks strategically. Whether those thoughts are written into a formal plan is of only secondary value.

The wisdom of Sun Tzu offers some guidance in how to approach a situation strategically. The venerable general offered five assessments that every leader should understand—that is, five elements of thinking strategically: "the way, weather, the terrain, the leadership, and discipline."[2] We'll look at how each of these contributes to the modern organization and the ability to think strategically.

The Way

In the military sense, the "way" represents the importance of making sure that all the troops understand and buy into the overarching goals of the conflict. You can liken this to our earlier discussion of vision except that here we are talking in much more specific terms about the need for the goals of those who follow to become congruent with the goals of those who lead. This is the hallmark of good management in any stage of change and an absolute necessity in the formulative environment of the Emerging stage. When the "way" is firmly established in people's minds and hearts, they can sustain a high level of commitment and loyalty regardless of the impact of change. In Sun Tzu's words, "When people have the same aim as the leadership they will share death and share life, without fear of danger."[3]

The Weather

Wars have been lost due to a lack of understanding of how weather can affect the ability of the army to carry out the battle plan. A good strategy therefore takes into account the seasons of the year.

2. Ibid.
3. Ibid, p. 99.

Thinking strategically requires developing a sense of anticipation and thus preparing for change, realizing that it is inevitable. We'll talk more about the value of information in the actual process of strategic planning, where emphasis is placed on continually monitoring the plan and changing it in response to the environment.

The Terrain

Naturally an army must travel, whether on foot, horse, tank, or other means. The distance, obstacles, and opportunities that may be encountered will affect the success of the battle plan.

Knowledge of conditions in the external setting as well as within the organization is a critical dimension of strategic thinking. Managers who have their ear to the ground are able to keep in touch with strengths, weaknesses, threats, and opportunities—the database for dealing with change.

Leadership

We'll talk at length about the application of leadership skills in the other stages of the change continuum, but mention of it here is useful. Leaders who understand strategic thinking become skilled in human behavior and recognize that sensitivity to the needs of others is the key. Ethical and moral behavior also translates into good "followership," which is crucial to surviving and then thriving in the Emerging stage.

Discipline

Strategic thinking must encompass an organized approach to implementing the battle plan. Much of the research suggests that one side of the brain is responsible for analytical thinking and the other for more creative pursuits. To deal with change effectively, both sides must be put into use. There must be an analytical focus on facts and figures. Then intuitive insights must establish the less obvious relationships between those facts and figures. In this sense the concept of strategizing takes on the nature of both art and science. The process of strategic planning puts these two poles together and provides the battle plan, which can be communicated throughout the ranks.

Strategic Planning: Turning Ideas into Actions

Strategic planning is best defined as the technical skill of translating thoughts into actions. It is the battle plan itself, the road map to guide the organization toward accomplishing its vision. Any number of steps can be concocted to represent the process, but it really boils down to answering four key questions:

1. What internal strengths and weaknesses and external threats and opportunities will affect our achieving our vision?
2. What are the key factors for success in the emerging business climate, and how should we measure them?
3. What specific targets should we set that will directly contribute to our vision?
4. What actions should we take? By when and who in the organization will be accountable for their implementation?

Answering each of these questions entails specific activities that can shed light on a lot of other facets of organizational life. The one that should be stressed in our examination of these activities is the opportunity for a breadth of involvement of various stakeholders. That involvement is not only essential to a good end product but will do wonders for the implementation of plans down the road.

Internal Strengths/Weaknesses And
External Threat/Opportunities

In many respects, the information gathered about the environment that the organization is operating in (and will operate in) is what makes planning strategic. In commonsense terms the possibilities for the future will be determined by the ability to respond to the conditions that exist. Once you understand the difference between where you want to go and where you are, you can set goals to move you in the right direction. You need to know the state of affairs inside the organization, as well as what is and will be happening in the marketplace and among those who use your product or service. Here are some of the sources for internal information:

• *Discussions with employees.* Often this is the last place we go to get data, but in fact it can prove to be one of the best. Employees at all levels know a lot about what's going on but seldom have a chance to give any meaningful input. Additionally, their involvement from the start in any new direction will build commitment for further development of objectives and actions.

• *Assessment interviews.* External consultants are an excellent resource for asking questions, especially if morale is low or top management does not have the rapport necessary to get straightforward answers. You must always be careful when using outside resources, but if they are highly skilled, they can get people to open up in ways that insiders would find difficult to do. Whether they do individual or small group interviews, the data can be invaluable in painting a clear picture of the workplace dynamics and how they will affect future efforts.

• *Attitude surveys.* If the climate isn't conducive to open discussion (common for the culture of the Emerging stage), written questionnaires can be used. The questions must be open-ended so as to beg a descriptive response. Asking, "Are things going well in your department?" is not as useful as asking, "What aspects of your department's operation could be enhanced?" It's also a good idea to include space for additional comments in case there are other issues that can be touched upon by the person responding.

Information on external conditions may seem easier to come by, but you'll have to make sure the information is applicable to your own situation. There are innumerable sources for demographic information (social statistics), but much of it may not be relevant to understanding your customers, constituents, or direct competitive forces. Broad trends in politics, technology, the economy, and the like may not be as meaningful as interacting with people in your own business environment. Some of the prime sources for external information follow:

▪ *Discussions with suppliers.* Those who provide you with resources are an excellent place to begin. They must develop an appreciation for what's going on in the marketplace because their own survival depends on it. They can share trends in customer preferences and pending changes in laws, policies, or regulations. An added benefit is that good supplier relationships and their knowledge of your operational demands can be a major strategic weapon.

▪ *Discussions with customers.* This should be the first source to come to mind, but organizations too seldom take advantage of the direct input from those who use their products or services. People will certainly tell you what they like, what they don't like, and why. The focus group process is a good approach because it allows you to compare the responses from a range of sources on a variety of issues.

▪ *Competitive analysis.* It is especially useful (and highly strategic) to examine what indirect competitors are thinking about. Indirect competitors are those who are not in your industry but whose product or service could replace yours in meeting the needs of your own customers. In the Emerging stage, this type of analysis can prevent early extinction or open up new markets.

■ *Discussions with employees*. Your own employees are an untapped source of information. You may be surprised at the knowledge of support staff (clerical, custodial, receptionists, and the like) on the movements in the environment that could signal the emergence of trouble or an opportunity. Employees at the working level of the organization have a firsthand exposure to changes in habit patterns, tastes, or preferences.

Once you begin to hear the same story being told from different sources, you will know something strategic is in the air. The ability to read the signals in the environment and then to develop strategies to capitalize on them is not only important in the Emerging stage but a hallmark of excellent organizations in general.

Key Factors for Success

The next aspect of the process is to translate the internal and external data you've gathered into direction for the organization. The cumulative effect of winning the major battles is that you win the war. What the Emerging organization has to discover is exactly what battles it should be fighting. In any endeavor, there will be anywhere from three to seven key factors for success. They represent the skills, capabilities, leverage points, or competitive advantages that will spell success in the business environment.

We'll use McDonald's as an example. When the concept of fast food was in its infancy McDonald's, as an Emerging company, focused on cleanliness, consistent quality, reasonable prices, local access, and competent service as the key factors for success. As simple as these might seem, they have become the criteria by which virtually all fast food is judged. Note also the number of competitors that *don't* measure up to McDonald's in these obvious traits. This is the power of key factors for success.

There is no magical formula you can use to arrive at these factors. Quite typically, when you get thorough answers to the first questions on the internal and external environment, key factors may surface. There is not quite as much opportunity for broad involvement here compared with other phases of the process. A good exercise for the top management team, though, is to spend a few hours sharing the environmental data and brainstorming. The only limitation that an Emerging organization may have is if it's a start-up venture, with little experience in the business or operation. Otherwise key factors for success should not be difficult to extrapolate from the institutional memory of an established organization.

Targets Contributing to the Vision

"Strategic objectives" is just a fancier way of saying "the identification of the specific accomplishments that need to be achieved in line with the key factors." Some also refer to this element of strategic planning as goal setting, but don't let the semantics trouble you. Whatever you want to call it, here are a few guidelines that will ensure the value of the concepts:

1. *Make sure they are reasonable targets.* Too often we set our sights beyond reality. Stay within the capabilities of the organization, and play to its strengths as a way of stretching those capabilities.

2. *Make sure they are measurable.* If one of the key factors has to do with operating efficiency, you might be tempted to use "increase efficiency and effectiveness" as a target. It sounds great, but how do you know when you've done it? If instead the target is "keep fixed costs at 20 percent of revenue," this guideline will make a tremendous contribution to efficiency and provide a way to measure it as well.

3. *Make sure they have a time frame.* Include a specific date as a way of expressing targets. This will be a big help when you develop action steps to reach them. Time frames also help in assessing the reasonableness of the entire plan.

You'll want to make sure that you cover all of the bases. An organization in the Emerging stage must fill the gap between where it wants or needs to be in the future and where it is now. Taken together, targets should accomplish this.

Action Steps

The most crucial aspect of strategic planning is when you actually commit to doing something. This is much less strategic and more operational, but it's amazing to discover the number of instances when a good strategic direction failed to achieve any notable results because the planning fell apart. Even more disturbing is the fact that the planning falls apart so often because of a lack of clarity and specificity over exactly **what** action was to have been taken, **who** was to get it done, and **when** it was to be have been completed. Consistency is achieved only by writing these things down and sticking with them.

Good action step formulation begins with the time frames established by the targets. From there it is simply a matter of working backward to the present. For example if a target is to be accomplished by December 1995, this becomes the starting point for planning. You would then spell out the sequence of events that would lead up to that terminal point.

The dates that are established also set in motion the periodic review of the action steps and the evaluation of the overall plan. This is what creates the iterative feature of good strategic planning. There is a fallacious notion that a strategic plan should not change, that it is somehow predictive. Just the opposite is true. There may be something fatally wrong with a plan that does not undergo periodic updating and revision. The environment is never static.

Moving beyond the Emerging Stage

The notion of anticipating change will be the most pressing need in the Emerging stage and the most compelling result of the strategic planning process. While the ultimate goal is to build this mode of thinking into the way you do business, the initial emphasis will usually be on generating the plan itself. Sometimes the most important output from strategizing is not so much the insight into where you're headed in the future, but where you are now. In the words of Sun Tzu, "so it is said if that if you know others and know yourself, you will not be imperiled in a hundred battles. If you do not know others but know yourself you will win and lose one. If you do not know others and do not know yourself you will be imperiled in every single battle."[4]

4. Ibid., p. 99.

Five

Organizing in The Expanding Stage: The Culture of The Machine

Production is not the application of tools to materials but logic to work.

Peter Drucker, management guru

The growth and development of an organization is not necessarily a linear process. In fact, some of the most successful businesses sprang from accidents rather than from planning. Ivory, the immortal soap product by Procter & Gamble, is an example. Customers have been enamored of the fact that Ivory floats. What most people don't realize is that that particular property was the result not of consumer research or strategic planning but of a worker's falling asleep on the job. When the air hose fell into the vat and put bubbles in the mixture, the only thing to do was to cut it up into bars and try to salvage it somehow. The novelty of floating soap was such a hit that the company began to produce it on purpose.

Change should cause us to appreciate the organic nature of the workplace, but in fact it does just the opposite. Stability and structure are always important, but in the Expanding stage they become mandatory. To be successful in this stage is to be a well-oiled apparatus with the role of each component clearly spelled out.

This so-called Culture of the Machine can be difficult to achieve, even with a systems approach and a functional orientation to work. In reality, the focus of most organizations (and especially those that survive the Emerging stage) is on the wrong things. Few have established clarity as to their performance. For example, although most performance appraisals purport to provide feedback on what the individual has accomplished over a period of time, it is more likely that they comment on how an employee approaches the job rather than what he or she produces through it. In the worst case, we measure attitudinal dimensions of this performance, such as "initiative" or "motivation." I am not suggesting that those aren't important features of a job; it's just that they aren't measurable, nor do they necessarily indicate that anything useful was produced by the employee.

The idea of a "machine" culture may sound routinized and impersonal, but as we examine it, you'll see the value of being able to streamline the production of work and to bring balance to the growth that the organization may be experiencing at this stage.

When You're Not Set Up to Serve

Knee-Jerk Reactions

Coming out of the Emerging stage, a successful organization is likely to experience one of two possible futures. The first is that under the prospective pressure of a shrinking market or the potential of increased competition, the organization decides to focus on ways to boost productivity, decrease its costs, or both. The more common scenario, though, is the second, when the strength of its products and services, or the buoyancy of the market it does business in, sustain its success regardless of what it does operationally. This is the age-old adage of the product's selling itself. No matter what the organization does or doesn't do, success seems to follow it.

It's hard to argue with success, but this ultimately leads to a lack of attention to the details of management systems, procedures, and processes. Human nature being what it is, it's difficult to justify taking certain actions when things are going well. The problem is that the Expanding stage signals the presence of change and a clear threat to continued success. Without an understanding of key factors for success at this stage, most organizations meet this threat with a variety of responses that often do more harm than good. One of those responses is a denial that change is even posing a threat. It can be hard to admit that the emphasis on strategy needs to be broadened by looking at how you do things. The consequences of this response are obvious. Another typical reaction is to fiddle with the organization chart, under the assumption that by moving things around, better results can be achieved. Unfortunately, the organization usually ends up doing the same things. Instead of reexamining the way operations are being approached, the tendency is simply to reorganize, hoping that a new configuration will make a difference. This is tantamount to rearranging the deck chairs on the *Titanic*.

Structure and Strategy

Expanding-stage entities often find themselves in need of a systemic approach to their operations that allows them to take full advantage of their strategic direction. When operations are not synchronized, the value of strategy is undercut; in some cases, strategy can be rendered useless. The primary thrust of banking institutions, for example, had always been in lending money to businesses. Operating services such as cash management were seen as add-ons to the basic lending function. The strategy, therefore, was to expand marketing efforts and reach customers through an extensive network of branches. Then in the mid-1970s, the industry began to undergo the metamorphosis that is evident today. New technology and a downturn in the economy began to change the focus subtly from lending to cash management and other operating services that helped customers maximize their flow of funds. Banks that had invested heavily in branches tried to stay competitive, but they simply were not set up to serve.

In today's business environment, downsizing has become a preferred antidote to a variety of ills. What happens too often is that costs *are* reduced and labor *is* trimmed, but there is no identifiable increase in profits or productivity. This is mainly due to a panic response toward change as the entity in the Expanding stage fails to link its structural changes with its strategic direction. Structure and strategy must always complement each other. Although the emphasis here will be on the need to redefine how works gets done, we are ever mindful of the larger purposes toward which the work is aimed.

The Problem with How Things Are Done

What features does the Culture of the Machine provide that are useful in this stage? Let's answer that by summarizing the typical deficiencies observed in the Organizing phase:

- *There is no concept of the organization as a system.* Activities are carried out in a fast and furious manner, but they aren't linked together to form a whole. People who perform these activities lack an overall appreciation for how their piece contributes toward the completed puzzle.
- *The specific outputs of job functions are unclear.* The lack of clarity stems from the absence of clear measurements. Certainly the most important things frequently cannot be quantified, yet each employee must know what his or her function should produce, not just what the responsibilities are.
- *The inputs needed to produce the desired results are inadequate.* Whether it's the lack of timely, accurate, informa-

tion or substandard raw materials, results can never be achieved without quality inputs.

- *There is no consistent review and evaluation of progress.* It's hard to improve operations when you're not sure how well or poorly you're doing.
- *The role and function of people becomes confusing.* No matter what level of technology is being used, it all comes back to people. The dysfunction of operational processes takes a human toll. Low morale, uncertain motivation, and a higher level of frustration can be anticipated.

If you consider any common machine, you might identify a number of properties:

- No matter how complex the machine is, all of its parts function together to perform the work.
- Each part has its own unique role, no matter how large or small that part might be; there is no confusion over that role and no destructive competition with the other parts.
- The machine has both clear outputs and the right inputs.
- The ingredients needed to fuel the machine's work are of the right quality and quantity.
- When working properly, the machine will deliver the same results on a more or less consistent basis.
- The machine requires maintenance. It can always be fixed once it breaks down, but a better idea is to perform preventive maintenance—a regular check of all of the machine's pars and functions to extend its useful life and level of performance.
- At some point in the sequence of the operation of the machine, people will have to know what to do. Sometimes their role may be as simple as to turn it on or off. In other instances, they may have to interact with the machine in order for the work to get done.

These same dimensions are required to establish a culture that will thrive in the Expanding stage. We'll talk specifically about how to achieve this culture, but here are the highlights:

1. Create linkages between the overall strategy of the organization and the outputs that need to be produced.
2. Design and redesign systems, processes, and procedures to produce those outputs in the most efficient and economical fashion possible.
3. Develop mechanisms that allow you to stay in touch with the changing needs of internal and external customers.
4. Remove interferences that prohibit employees from recreating systems, procedures, and processes.
5. Align reporting relationships to obtain consistent, timely, and comprehensive feedback on the adequacy of the operational structure.

I hope the idea of a Culture of the Machine is sounding less regimented and impersonal. The metaphor suggests that the parameters of organizational performance are spelled out in such a way that the organization functions like a machine. When the required elements are present, this culture can be one of the most exciting to be a part of. Though not as dynamic and freewheeling as the Emerging stage, there is ample opportunity for creativity and ingenuity. Of all of the tools that are available, the ideas in the field of quality management have ready application in the Expanding stage. The emphasis in quality is placed on understanding how work is done and on recasting operational methods.

The Quality Game

A Brief History

At any stage of change, discipline is required. If the Culture of War brings discipline to the way an organization thinks, then the Culture of the Machine brings added discipline to the way it acts. It is for precisely this reason that quality management concepts have a profound impact in the Expanding stage.

Probably no other management tool is receiving as much attention these days as total quality management (TQM). Neither has any other management tool been as much misapplied either.

TQM as we know it today was actually invented in the United States, although the success of Japanese organizations in the late 1970s and throughout the 1980s causes most newcomers to the subject to attribute it to the Japanese. The reason is that in the early 1950s, the proponents of quality management could not get U.S. companies to embrace the ideas. Just after World War II, whatever the United States made, the rest of the world bought, without much concern over quality. In fact, the notion of managing the adherence to specifications or production guidelines was never even thought of as the responsibility of management until the 1920s, when G. S. Radford penned the revolutionary work, "The Control of Quality in Manufacturing."[1]

Because of their dismal situation following their defeat, the Japanese had little to turn to and went after TQM with a passion. What they learned to do was in many ways pure common sense. It was their commitment to taking a long-term prospective in implementing that common sense that has made all the difference. The logic of people like W. Edwards Deming, Arnaud Feigenbaum, Joseph Juran, and more recently Philip Crosby can be summarized in a few key points:

- All work is a process, meaning that you can diagram and study the inputs, steps that add value to those inputs, and the outputs received by the user.
- There is a natural variability built into any process and the required tasks, independent of the skills of the person (or group of people) performing the task.
- Continuous improvements in quality (depending on how it should be measured) are attained by reducing that variability through continuous improvement of the process.

1. (New York: Ronald Press, 1922).

- Those who are associated with the input side (suppliers), the valued-added tasks (workers), and users of the output (customers) need to work together in designing a process or in improving one.
- The environment of the organization must be conducive to communicating across departmental boundaries, between levels, and with external stakeholders.

As straightforward as this appears U.S. businesses have had a great deal of difficulty in making it work. It is imperative, especially in the Expanding stage, to understand the last point thoroughly or else the benefits of the preceding ones will never be obtained.

Cultivating a Quality Culture

One of the worst habits that organizations can develop is chasing after each new management fad and hailing it as the answer to all of its troubles. This is nowhere more evident than with the current TQM craze that is sweeping across the American management landscape. The message that is being promoted says all of the right things, but the implementation can be quite different. In essence, we try to appropriate all of the mechanics of quality management without making a real commitment to cultivate a culture in which the ideas can flourish.

If we don't acknowledge the stage of organizational change, then any management tool that is used will deliver less than optimal results. TQM is well suited for the Expanding stage because of the ability to form a culture that is ready and able to make the kind of changes that quality necessitates. Quality management is a valuable tool, but it cannot be implemented in the same way the Japanese did or without factoring in the stage of change. Just as there are large cultural differences between the American and the Japanese workplace, so are there differences based on where organizations are in the change cycle. Without this recognition, there are a number of common failings in trying to apply the benefits of quality management.

Employees can tell when there is a genuine commitment by top management to change the culture of the workplace from one based on internal competition to one based on consensus decision making and shared values. These new values can be instilled during the Expanding stage quite easily, but only with premeditated action.

Barriers between departments or work units whose cumulative efforts are responsible for delivering the particular product or services are another culture phenomenon. The presence of "fiefdoms" or "turf" is common to our American scene. The premise of quality management, however, suggests that people will be willing to open up the operations of the areas they supervise so that processes and procedures can be studied and changed. The protectionism that is the more likely reaction can forestall the most sophisticated quality efforts.

Finally, there is a cultural reliance on formal structure— the one described by organization charts and position descriptions, most of them less than an accurate depiction of reality. We talk and believe as if the formal structure is getting the work done, when in practice it just doesn't happen that way. Often, in fact, the formal structure gets in the way of getting work done. By looking at the actual way that things happen, we can diagram and analyze procedures and processes in order to make them more productive.

In the Expanding stage, much of this necessary work is easier because lines of authority and accountability are not yet entrenched, and the potential for effecting real teamwork is greatly enhanced. Teamwork is the bedrock of quality management.

The Truth about Teamwork

What Do We Really Mean?

It might appear that the idea of the Culture of the Machine might fly in the face of teamwork, but empirical results would say otherwise. For example, if you witness the performance of an accomplished athletic team or ballet company, you will notice first and foremost the precision with which the individuals carry out their movement. Obviously the game plan and the roles of the individuals are clear, and they have devoted a fair amount of practice time to meshing the two. In fact, outstanding football or basketball teams are often referred to as a "machine" because of these characteristics.

It would be hard for anyone who has been a part of any group to deny that teamwork isn't a wonderful attribute. What is interesting, though, is to probe exactly what we mean by teamwork and how it looks in the workplace. Technically, *teamwork* refers to a cooperative effort to achieve a common goal. But what is the goal, and how do we express *cooperative?* In practice, both are interpreted on an individual basis, so there is room for tremendous differences in interpretation. Being able to create a single definition is the most critical issue in quality management.

If we are to reap the benefits of quality management, we have to settle on a single goal for the workplace and establish an environment whereby people can function as team. The experts may have found the answer when they stress that the goal of everyone is to satisfy the needs of customers. In fact, true teamwork can be realized when employees also see each other as customers. This means that before you sit down to perform your particular job function you consider the needs of those who will be using the output you produce. In fact, you might even go to that person and ask, "What form should the output take in order for you to do your job more effectively?" If everyone agrees about this philosophy, then the quality that the external customer receives will have to be improved as well. Making the customer's satisfaction the common goal creates a dynamic team setting.

Then there's the issue of cooperation. One subtlety of work is that although we are divided into work units, most outputs to the customer represent the collaborative efforts of many units that may never interact with one another. Here the key is to create incentives that motivate teamwork on a grander scale. Most people feel inclined to work together, but there are often disincentives to doing so. For example, when the sharing of information across organizational boundaries is discouraged by the supervisor, teamwork grinds to a halt.

The premise of quality management says that the route to continuous improvement is through the system's being used to get the work done. Just as the goal is to satisfy customers, the incentive structure must reward the corporate improvements in the system rather than individual or departmental performance. We must be able to borrow from the best practices of those who have been successful in promoting teamwork but not lose sight of how to implement it in our own environment.

Transferring the Japanese Experience

Perhaps the most outstanding feature of the teamwork model as used by Japanese workers is the way in which the overall societal values provide support for it. For example, the idea of seeking individual recognition is foreign to the culture; rather, rewards are given on the basis of group performance. Another interesting notion is the importance of individuals doing their best to contribute to the team so as to avoid dishonor. In addition, the technical approach to team formulation and development in Japan almost guarantees success. These types of factors, coupled with more than forty years of concentrating on quality, make the experience of American organizations and that of the Japanese hard to compare.

Nevertheless, some ideas are transferable to the United States. Here is a prescription for creating the foundation for teamwork that is mandatory for success in using quality management in the Expanding stage:

1. *Motivate employees to become a part of problem-solving teams voluntarily.* Coercion is fine, but when you mandate teamwork, you violate the underlying principle. The focus of these teams also is important. If the feeling is that their purpose is just to talk about issues, it will be hard to generate participation. But if there is an opportunity to be actively involved in fixing things that aren't working, the response will be altogether different.

2. Orient employees to the mission and goals of the organization. It might seem an unnecessary step, but it usually isn't. Although most employees may know the mission and goals, it is likely that they haven't internalized them. They must if they are to grasp the importance of internal and external customers and of focusing on improving the system.

3. Train employees in the tools and techniques of problem solving. An effective team must have the skills to perform in its area of endeavor. There are a number of analytical and creative methods that can equip a group to function with a high level of expertise and confidence. In general, training should be an integral and ongoing part of any team effort.

4. Allow the team to develop. None of the preceding steps actually makes a team. Functioning as a team is an end result that must evolve. Under the proper conditions, that evolution is easy. Still, there are barriers that any group must pass through before becoming a team. The most critical is when they establish their own norms for roles, behaviors, and responsibilities. Once these are accomplished, a successful team will emerge.

You might remember back to the late 1970s when the quality circle movement attempted to impart much of the wisdom of teamwork Japanese style. It was a good idea, but it has some serious shortcomings in generating the motivation to continue the effort until it becomes part of the workplace culture and not just another program. In the Expanding stage, priority is placed on setting the stage for long-term viability. Being able to weave the quality concept into the fabric of the entity is a vital end result.

Building the Commitment to Do A Better Job

Kodak and Quality

In the mid-1980s, Kodak, the world-famous photographic products company, restructured its operations. Over the prior five to seven years, there had been rapid growth in the industry, followed by some serious shake-ups and an even more dramatic decrease in product life cycles. The company was standing on the threshold of the Expanding stage, and to remain competitive it would have to improve the efficiency of operations. The main goal was to create and recreate products that matched the needs of customers.

Management's first step was to take a closer look at the way they developed new products and find opportunities to improve it. This is the nuts and bolts of the Expanding stage. The effort to flowchart an operation and use teams to study its parameters is the only way to make improvements. If the customer evaluates quality as speed, ease of use, reliability, or durability, the process must be able to deliver just that. Even in an organization with multiple lines of business, being able to document processes like product development enables it to create a standardized methodology that can be adjusted to suit different situations. Thus, a company like Kodak gets the best of both worlds—a dependable, predictable routine that has flexibility based on customer needs. This is the hallmark benefit of the Culture of the Machine.

The second step was to turn over product development responsibility to a team structure—not just the traditional product development people but representatives from the full range of functions leading to manufacture of a new product. Obviously this speaks to a significant alteration in culture as well as proper training to allow the team to function effectively, but the results are well worth it. Many automobile manufacturers, among others, have seen the benefits of this strategy; it generates an unparalleled pride in workmanship.

Next, barriers between departments were systematically dismantled to allow for the cross-pollination necessary to make the structure work. The main benefit here was that a new openness helped to decrease the experimentation time for new-product ideas. These changes required a fair amount of investment in materials and equipment, and there were other factors to consider, such as how to administer compensation, incentives, and career development. The personnel and human resources management systems must be built around the way work gets done, not the other way around.

Finally the loop was closed when Kodak set up pilot facilities to allow the teams to bring the new-product ideas to the point at which customers could try them before going into full-scale production. All too often we experiment on the customer and suffer huge losses if the product or service fails to meet expectations, so this was an important step for Kodak in the quality process. This way the probability of catastrophic failure is much lower. The willingness to invest in the long term and to provide the support mechanisms for teams to thrive will always pay off. In the Expanding stage, it is crucial that the benefits of these principles be stressed.

Selling Quality Management

To round out this examination of the Expanding stage and the application of the principles of quality management, it's helpful to zero in on the key factors that will motivate an organization to embrace it wholeheartedly. While you can never make people want to do so, the suggestion is that if the incentives are powerful enough, the ideas can become anchored in workplace practices.

I've alluded to the notion of the system as the real culprit in improving quality, and the assertion stands. A further implication, though, is that since top management controls the system for the most part, the power to improve really is vested in them. W. Edwards Deming created a stir in the 1950s when he attributed 85 percent of all organizational deficiencies to upper management.[2] In 1992 his revised statistics suggested the figure was closer to 96 percent![3] The threat posed by lukewarm commitment from top management is obvious. If top management can demonstrate its commitment to allowing the culture to change, there is no limit to what employees will be willing to do for the future of the organization.

2. *Out of Crisis* (Cambridge, Mass.: MIT, 1986).
3. American Association of School Administrators Seminar, Arlington, Va., March, 1992.

One of the first objections to the investment in quality is the cost, and it does take time, money, and energy to cover all of the bases. But there is a rumor circulating in management circles that says that you have to spend substantially more to produce and deliver a higher-quality product or service. In reality, it is just the contrary. One of the most famous quality stories is that of the Ford Motor Company's Taurus automobile. As the tale goes, Ford was down to its last $3 billion, and the division that was responsible for producing Ford's last-ditch effort to revive the company called in the quality gurus. Their recommendations entailed massive teamwork, unheard-of committee participation, and the like. The result was one of the best cars Ford has ever built and an ever more unheard of $450 million budget savings! With outcomes of this proportion, quality management can be very easy to sell.

A machine's useful life is extended by preventive maintenance. Part of the expense equation is an important concern for entities in the Expanding stage. If you think about it, it costs the same amount of money to produce a defective product as it does one that works. A defective product, however, costs more because of the need for scrapping, repair, or rework. Worse yet is the loss of business from defective merchandise.

When an organization begins to tolerate anything less than excellence, it is on its way to decay and ultimately destruction. This course becomes evident when inordinate amounts of attention are given to catching problems after they have occurred and to fixing things after they are broken. It is the preventive nature of quality management that is the biggest gain in this stage of change.

The actions that are part of the Culture of the Machine represent the opportunity to sustain the success created in the previous stage. Far more than regimentation, it establishes a setting in which creativity can be exercised and where the very things that rob employees of the joy of creating can be dealt with before they become the norm. Most important, this culture begins to orient the organization to look outside itself and see the needs of customers, a skill that will become increasingly more valuable.

Six

Listening in The Maturity Stage: The Culture Of the Organism

The underdog in many products can pick and choose where it wants to hit the giant. The giant, by contrast, must defend itself everywhere.

George Leach, president, Colgate-Palmolive

The priority of responding to the external environment increases by an order of magnitude in the Maturity stage. The failure to do so can signal the onset of a lethargy that will cause an organization to fall asleep at the wheel. On the other hand, the positive momentum that can emanate from the prior stages can make the Maturity phase an especially fruitful time in the cycle of change. If the Emerging-stage priority for strategic planning and the Expanding stage's lesson on customer focus have been applied, the Maturity stage can be extremely profitable.

The Culture of the Organism used to describe the nature of change in this stage has some similarities to the Culture of the Machine. An organism is a collection of parts and processes that work together just as a machine has components that function in concert. The difference is that an organism is a living thing, not an inanimate object. This notion of a living thing speaks to the priority in the Maturity stage for reenergizing in an effort to ward off the predictable hardening of the arteries that lies ahead. In fact, the more successful the organization has been, the greater the tendency is for this hardening. People get used to doing things in a certain way, and if it has been working well, they see little incentive to make any changes. Additionally, the standardized methods that worked in the Expanding stage turn to rend us in Maturity. Repetitious success degenerates the need to question how the work is being done, and we no longer think of coworkers as internal customers. Very slowly and imperceptibly, the external customer becomes the servant of our systems, procedures, and processes. In simple terms, we begin to lose touch with the basics of the business and no longer listen to those whom we are supposedly in business to satisfy.

The antidote for the ills of the Maturity stage is a large dose of the marketing mentality: the understanding that it is everyone's job to learn about, listen to, and satisfy customers. Beyond the notion of quality management, we learn to track the wants and needs of customers and even to educate and influence them around those needs. It is a time also to merge the broad concepts of strategic planning that may have become blurred with actions in the marketplace. The Culture of the Organism is one in which this mentality breathes new life into a setting in which change threatens to shorten the life cycle of success that many employees may have come to expect as a norm.

McDonald's and Marketing

A Master at Managing Change

Perhaps no other business has exemplified the Culture of the Organism better than McDonald's or has ridden the crest of the Maturity stage for as long. The story is still being written as McDonald's continues to lead the way in the fast food industry. If you look back at the company's history, you will also be able to see how it managed the prior stages of change in a masterful way. Back in the early 1960s, Ray Kroc was a man with not much capital but a vision. He painted a compelling picture of not just his business idea's success potential but that of the concept of fast food.

Not many people thought fast food would become a mainstay of the American public's tastes, but Kroc made it so. As mentioned previously, his strategy focused on maintaining consistent quality, good service, and reasonable prices—three things that almost any service organization would love to do. The strategy also consisted of an aggressive plan to build the most extensive distribution network of any type.

Whether you are in Portland, Oregon; Des Moines, Iowa; or the Bronx, a Big Mac is still a Big Mac—right? That's because the company has mastered the concept of process improvement and provides outstanding training and support for franchise operators. The company spends a great deal of time studying the way the work is done and improving customer service. What really makes McDonald's special, though, is its keen marketing sense. You might not think of McDonald's as a marketer in the same way that you would a consumer goods company, but if you watch its actions, it becomes obvious that the company possesses awesome capabilities in this area. For one, it really listens to the needs of the marketplace. While McDonald's seems to prefer not to come out with too many different products, some regional tastes are reflected in the sandwich menus. And a couple of years ago when the environmental furor over polystyrene containers erupted, McDonald's was the first to respond. When health considerations brought criticism over the fat content of fast foods, it was the first to offer "lite" menus and salads. I could go on and on singing McDonald's praises.

The heart of the matter in this marketing prowess is not necessarily having a huge marketing department of spending a lot of money on advertising and promotion. These things help, but there is one detail around which everything else must revolve: knowledge of the customer.

The Niche

Maturity-stage organizations can hang around a long time if they can lock on to a part of the market where it is difficult for others to compete with them. In marketing jargon, this is called a "niche." Being able to identify and maintain a niche position requires superlative knowledge of the needs, habits, and behaviors of the customers. McDonald's may have found an eternal niche by its concentration on children as their primary customer.

If you've ever watched the parents of small children in a fancy restaurant, you can sense their discomfort and trepidation. They feel as if no one wants them there. The frowns, the whispers, and the less-than-excited greeting by the maitre'd are all signs that perhaps they aren't really wanted there. In a lot of cases, those parents' fears are justified: they *aren't* wanted. No one would be so insulting as to say it, but children can affect the ambience of a nice restaurant. They spill things. They want to pour catsup on delicacies. They are loud.

Now consider the contrasting picture of parents being pulled through the Golden Arches by beaming children. Probably more than the desire for the food (although the french fries are always a big hit), the youngsters probably want a Happy Meal or to collect the newest trinket being offered. This is a pure lesson in marketing that should not be overlooked: more than any other restaurant or fast food establishment, the message is that it's not only okay to bring kids here but in fact McDonald's loves to have them! Even though they don't pay the check or provide the transportation, kids play a major role in the buying decision: determining what restaurant the family goes to. This role qualifies them as a primary customer.

Think about it. Not only does the menu offer attractive food to children, but the entire place is childproof. The countertops are stainless steel; the floors are mosaic tile, so when a milkshake spills, the wet vacuum comes out and cleans it right up. The chairs and tables are bolted to the floor, and the pictures are tightly secured to the walls. It's virtually impossible to destroy a McDonald's. Should the little ones become restless, many locations have an equally indestructible playground. McDonald's clearly understands some of the key aspects of marketing and the importance of understanding customers.

The Power of Follow-Through

In addition to this targeted emphasis on the customer, Mc-Donald's has built the management and organizational structure to support its marketing efforts. The ability to follow through from basic customer research to the training of counter staff is what it's all about. Consider this contrasting tale of another food establishment.

The York Steakhouse used to be a popular cafeteria-style eating place in the Maryland area. One Friday night in the fish-and-seafood-oriented town of Baltimore, a long line of people had formed to place their orders. The waitress standing beside the billboard menu had one of those "I-wish-I-were-someplace-else-tonight" looks on her face. An elderly woman with apparently failing eyesight came up to place her order. She squinted at the menu board and began to ask some typical customer questions about the evening's fare, including, "Is the salmon a steak or a filet?" to which the not-happy-to-be-here waitress replied, "I don't know, lady, I only work here." The woman's combination of hesitance to order and polite insistence on getting an answer to her question prompted the waitress to consent to asking Brenda, an even-unhappier-to-be-here waitress who was preparing salads at the other end of the conveyor. She called out, "Brenda! Is the salmon a steak?" to which Brenda responded with a loud and frustrated response, "No, you fool, it's fish!!!!"

This story always elicits chuckles, but it's very sad from the perspective of this book. No doubt somewhere there's a York Steakhouse boardroom complete with wood paneling

and marbletop table around which executives talk about
strategic plans, market share, and competitive advantage.
There are probably easel sheets displaying business goals and
objectives that a consultant helped facilitate. These executives
probably have a clear idea of what it takes to create and hold
on customers, *but no one told Brenda!* No one, of course, can
blame her for what she apparently wasn't trained and motivated to do.

Now consider McDonald's again. Its leaders understand
that the best marketing is that which is illustrated by the
people who touch customers every day. The principles are
simple to understand but require a concentrated effort to
apply.

Marketing 101

The Expectation of Value

Perhaps the simplest way to express the essence of marketing
is to define it as the idea of having an organized effort to
attract and hold on to customers. Successful organizations in
the Maturity stage have always understood this definition,
though they may not have been as conscious about its application as the changing environment demands. If the product or
service has pretty much sold itself or if the track record in the
industry has always been good, it's easy to lose touch with this
definition.

Customers themselves don't often have a conscious understanding of why they are buying. Charles Revson of
Revlon put it best when he said, "In the manufacturing plant
we sell cosmetics but to the marketing people the product that
we offer is 'hope.' " Within this quotation lies the first principle of marketing: customers do not buy products or services as
much as expectations of value. Getting in touch with this value
perception is important because it is a key to staying current
with preferences and buying habits.

The best marketers meet customers' needs accurately and

consistently. Through the expectation of value, they establish a buying incentive, which if properly triggered will usually result in a sale. The buying incentive then becomes the core strategy of their efforts, and all activities are designed to support it in the marketplace. Companies that have an insight into this value are able to maintain their competitive advantage longer. Competitive advantage is the basis on which a niche position is established.

This intersection between what the customer values and the ability to deliver is where marketing begins. If you can deliver that value better than the others, you possess competitive advantage. For example, if you want to send a package and it "absolutely, positively, has to be there overnight," what company would you probably consider as a solution to your problem? For many, it would be Federal Express. Its Memphis hub system enables it to meet the expectation of timely delivery better than just about any other carrier in a fiercely competitive industry.

Sensitivity to expectations of value can forestall the lethargy that comes with the Maturity stage. The tool manufacturer Black and Decker has a novel way of approaching the marketing aspects of its business. The division that makes electric drills speaks of its business as "selling holes." In other words, the customer doesn't really want a drill as much as the holes that the drill makes. This might sound simplistic, but in the competitive sense, there are lots of ways to make holes, including laser technology, creating the potential for indirect competitors to attract those customers.

Marketing Mechanics

Despite the proliferation of jargon that surrounds the marketing field, there are some basic mechanics that every organization should become conversant in. Let's talk about market segmentation, competitive analysis, marketing mix decisions, and marketing plans to gain some insight into their application.

Market Segmentation

Market segmentation basically means to divide up the universe of current and potential customers into groups based on characteristics that say something about their needs and buying habits. An organization in the Maturity stage will often find that its success has attracted competitors and its ability to be everything to everybody is severely limited. To maintain its edge, it will have to target customers more carefully and build plans based on their unique buying incentives. It may elect to serve any number of segments as far as its resources and ability to deliver what it has promised will allow.

Segments are distinguished by their common values and/or characteristics. In fact, segments can be established on various levels:

- *Geographics.* Sometimes where customers live present opportunities to understand their buying incentives. For example, efforts can be targeted at rural versus suburban markets, or potential customers can be attracted according to their zip code.

- *Demographics.* This most familiar basis of segmentation looks at social statistics, such as age, income, gender, and education. For example, in broadcasting, market segments are based on age categories such as "18–34" or "55 and over." Combined demographic characteristics are even more insightful. If you were marketing a magazine, you could target single women with graduate degrees aged 25–39 with an income of $35,000 and above.

- *Volume.* One of the common marketing philosophies is that the best source of new business is existing customers. By segmenting the market based on how much they use the product or service, an organization can increase its potential. Other volume characteristics might be response rates or performance.

- *Psychographic.* This newest segmentation approach is based on more subjective characteristics, such as social attitudes, life-style preferences, or other similar dimensions. The issue with psychographics is the potential for manipulating the customer by capitalizing on aspects of human weakness such as greed or envy to create demand for a product. This is an ethical question, not a conceptual one. Insights into buying habits based on these criteria can be extremely productive.

The Maturity-stage organization has only one major thing to fear: making mistakes that will give its competitors an entrée into the market. Segmentation is a valuable way of rationing scarce resources or avoiding competitive plunders.

Competitive Analysis

Understanding the competition requires data gathering and analysis of both direct and indirect competitors in order to get some insight into what their likely strategy will be. It's hard to outdo Michael Porter's contribution to the concept of competitive analysis.[1] His model picks out five forces that need to be looked at to be effective in dealing with competitors:

1. Rivalry among existing competitors.
2. Threat of new entrants, which can be met by making it difficult for them to gain access to distribution channels, pricing them out of market segments, and making it more expensive for customers to leave and do business with them.
3. The bargaining power of buyers.
4. The bargaining power of suppliers. The third and fourth forces refer to the impact that customer preferences and supplier threats can have on the product or service offered, as well as its quality, pricing, and packaging. This can be a little-noticed but powerful force to reckon with.

1. *Competitive Strategy* (New York: Free Press, 1980).

5. The threat of substitute products or services. This refers to indirect competitors and their ability to offer products that perform the same function.

This area should remind you of the previous discussion of strategic planning. There, the same kinds of questions were asked as benchmarks for looking at environmental trends. Competitive data in marketing, though, are more vital. There are only so many customers to go around, and waiting for them to come to you can be risky. Human service organizations, libraries, and even public schools present even greater challenges. These are places that have historically not had to worry much about marketing and never considered themselves to be in a competitive situation. But in recent years they have not only encountered competition but have seen the need to maintain their image in the face of critical publicity. Things sure are changing.

Marketing Mix Decisions

The marketing mix is actually a number of different decision points that support and implement the buying incentive for a given market segment or segments. Included in the mix are product and market research activities, distribution channel decisions, advertising, promotion, sales, and customer service. The emphasis on each depends on the type of business. The organization in the Maturity stage will likely have mastered some of these and possess potentially deadly deficiencies in others. A common area of deficiency is customer service. This is where the Culture of the Organism analogy becomes powerful. The key to vitality in this stage again is to listen to customers (as well as suppliers) to avoid the traps and pitfalls. Here are a number of customer service strategies that are useful at this point:

1. *Gain access to the top.* Customers feel they deserve to talk to the head honcho to get their questions answered or con-

cerns resolved. "Head honcho" is a relative concept, but it is clear that customers value at least the perception of this type of service.

2. *Remember, everyone is in charge of service.* You have probably experienced the frustration of seeing two or three employees at a retail establishment stand around in their own sales area chatting while you cool your heels looking for someone to wait on you. Sure, you appreciate that they have a system that they are following, but it seems that any one employee ought to be willing and able to help any customer spend money, regardless of department. In general, customers feel that anyone should be able to provide them with service.

3. *Follow up after the sale.* Whether it's an automobile or a charitable donation, the customer has been sold something and the best way to ensure, the person's happiness is to touch base after you've cashed the check. Many customers feel neglected by organizations that come on so exuberantly during the sales process but drop them like a hot potato after it's over. If you want to keep them coming back, show your appreciation for their choosing you over the competition. This is also one of the least expensive ways to gather information for new-product or service development as well as to evaluate the effectiveness of your entire marketing mix.

4. *Fix your failures fast.* One of the more disheartening aspects of customers is that it is much more difficult to gain their loyalty than it is to lose it. In fact, the overwhelming majority of dissatisfied customers will never say they're dissatisfied. They'll simply decide to do business somewhere else. Interestingly, they will tell lots of other people about their bad experience and warn them to stay away from you so the same thing won't happen to them.

You should know that a good two-thirds of them will remain loyal if you can resolve their problems quickly. One of the best examples is the mid-Atlantic region hardware chain Hechingers, which will give a prompt refund of any product purchased at any one of its stores with or without a receipt. Its leaders know that a little bit of service goes a long way toward gaining loyal and long-term customers.

5. *Reinforce good communications skills.* It should be obvious that good communications skills are essential, but they certainly aren't universal. In the earlier stages of change, organizations tend to treat customers with kid gloves, afraid to be unkind to them for fear of losing them. In the Maturity stage, there is a tendency to take them for granted. Employees should know that the customer is not always right; it's just they should treat them as if they are. Smiling (with face and voice), using their name, not putting them on hold for inordinate amounts of time, conversing with them while waiting for the terminal to come back up: these are ways to exhibit the proper communication techniques. It takes only one insulting or rude exchange to damage years of investment in a customer's loyalty.

6. *Turn a sale into a relationship.* This last point can make customer service an integral part of the overall marketing strategy. It is very expensive to drum up new business. The best source is existing customers. Here's a case in point. Nordstrom is a high-end department store that has some creative approaches to this idea of relationship. Let's suppose you purchase a couple of suits during the summer. The salesperson will note your size and style preferences, and when the fall season rolls around you might get a call saying that he or she put away few choice outfits during last month's sale that you might like. When you come down to the store (which you're likely to do), you'd see a bag under the counter with your name on it. Will you buy those outfits? Maybe. Maybe not. Regardless, you sure are impressed, and you feel as if someone really cared to take the time to think about your needs and to do something for you. That's the power of it. In this age of social security numbers and bar codes, all a customer really wants is to be treated like a human being, an individual, and to know that someone cares. This is a step beyond simple follow-up.

Marketing Plans

This is where it all comes together—where buying incentive and marketing mix become operationalized. Marketing plans are just like any other plans; they spell out actions and the timing of those actions. The easiest way to organize and remember the structure of marketing plans to think of the five P's: potential, product (or service), place, promotion, and price. Taken together they cover all of the steps in maximizing the value of a market segment. If you can answer the important questions in each of the P's, you can construct an effective plan:

Potential:
- How large is the segment? (dollar volume, number of customers, competitors)
- What barriers to competition exist or can be constructed?
- What buying incentive should be used as the core strategy?

Product:
- What features of the product or service should be stressed to support the core strategy?
- What features will provide the greatest competitive advantage?

Place:
- Where should the product be made available to customers?
- How should it be made available?
- How do we ensure that the product will be available when the customer wants it?

Promotion:
- How do we advertise the product?
- How do we organize the sales effort?
- How can we create the right image for the product in the mind of the customer?

Price:
- How much should the product cost in dollar terms?
- What other costs will the customer incur?
- What add-ons can be provided that will increase the value to the customer?

There are a lot more questions that you can add to each category. You may notice that selling is far down in the planning process. In the early stages, "marketing" and "selling" are thought of as synonymous, but in the Maturity stage, selling becomes the *result* of marketing. This is as good an indicator as any of the concept of a marketing mentality.

Removing the Blockages to Doing Business

The final concern of the Maturity-stage organization is to search for any aspect of the operation that makes it difficult for people to do business with you. This is the precursor to becoming mired in procedures at the expensive of the customer. If not caught now, it will become increasingly less likely that future problems in the change process can be avoided. Among the more common blockages, these are particularly troublesome to customers:

- Inconsistency between the promise and the delivery.
- Not being able to try it out before buying it.
- Too long a time span between order and receipt of a product.
- Complicated and time-consuming forms and other documentation.
- Hidden costs.
- Sales personnel who are pushy or lack in-depth product knowledge.
- Contact with multiple personnel, each of whom you must start at the beginning with.

A few words about the special concerns of service organizations are appropriate. The strategy here is to have the service provide a tangible impact—like any product that you can see and touch. Simply strengthening communications with the customer to let them know what they got from you and how good they feel about having gotten it can do the trick. This is where listening becomes vital in the Maturity stage. More frequent and extensive contact with customers provides the intelligence to reinforce the benefits they have derived from using your services.

You may notice that your local police force is out on the streets these days making contact with you and your neighbors, handing out their business cards, and reassuring you that your safety is their highest priority. They too have taken to marketing, realizing that your tax dollars buy their services. It's not a perfect correlation to the private sector but close enough that the same principles apply. When you go to polls and can pull the lever in favor of a tax increase that will fund more slots on the police force, you may remember the friendly face that showed up at your front door last month. What they have been able to accomplish is to make a service look like a product and to convince you to remain a loyal customer.

Last Chance to Manage Change

The message at the beginning of this chapter was that listening is the way to avoid lethargy and prolong the benefits of the Maturity stage. It needs to be repeated: *the Maturity stage is the last chance to manage change.* If you miss the opportunity, then from here on in, change manages you. That isn't necessarily a gloom-and-doom prophecy, but it does say that from here on in, you will spend more time bailing yourself out of problems than in enjoying your successes. Careful mastery of the Maturity stage leads to a recycling of the organization's efforts and return to the more youthful mind-set of strategic planning as we have seen here. The price of failure is then the reciprocal—when an organism stops moving, it will atrophy. As Quinn Spitzer, president of Kepner-Tregoe, the international training firm, once told me, "it is much easier to give birth than to perform a resurrection."[2] How true.

2. Conversation with author, September 1981.

Seven

Leading in The Entrenched Stage: The Culture Of The Journey

Managers are people who do things right and leaders are people who do the right things.

Warren Bennis, educator and writer

In the field of management, there exists a perpetual dichotomy, variously termed as the importance of balancing the emphasis on just getting the job done versus catering to the needs of people or juggling short-term operational concerns with the longer-term strategic issues. The two extremes come together in the discussion of the needs of an organization in the Entrenched stage. Many of the principles of organizational effectiveness that have been discussed previously now become embodied in the skills and abilities of people, often of *a* person—the leader of the company, the work unit, or the team. At any level and type of authority, we can talk about leadership. It's an elusive concept but one that is central to understanding this phase (as well as all others).

The Culture of the Journey is the analogy that paints a picture of the environment of the Entrenched organization and the character of leadership needed. First let's look at leadership. Imagine the climate of fifteenth-century Europe and the obstacles Columbus faced. The prevailing wisdom, as we all know, was that the earth was flat and nothing lay beyond the horizon but danger and destruction. Once Columbus convinced the powers that be that their paradigms were flawed, his greatest feat was in convincing other sailors to go along with him. It's one thing to risk your mind-set and a few thousand dollars. It's another to risk your life on someone else's supposition of what may exist beyond the known realm. If you consider this factor, the ability to convince people to take a chance and look beyond their limitations was a startling feat. It was perhaps even more startling than the seamanship skills that got them to the Caribbean.

The lack of flexibility and frequently the sheer impact of size can make it difficult to envision success. It is also possible that a string of unfortunate events in the external business setting can create the Entrenched stage for an organization, as we witnessed with the U.S. automobile industry in the mid-1970s. The Entrenched stage is not the end of the cycle. It is more like a wall that must be scaled.

Addressing Vulnerabilities

This would be a good time to note that these stages do not always present perilous situations; rather, you need to stay tuned in and on the right channel in order to avoid problems and to see the opportunities presented at each juncture of the change cycle. Still, that becomes far more difficult at this stage. The Entrenched organization is one of the most difficult to manage and lead. To turn around a huge ship, an ocean liner let's say, you have to begin to move the rudder a long time before you actually plan to turn.

Dealing with Competition:
Diversification and Development

Size and complexity are not bad, but maintaining them requires tremendous diversification, delegation, and a serious commitment to communicating inside and outside. The cosmetic company Maybelline, which runs number two in the industry behind Revlon, has taken an axe over the past few years to its line of nearly 600 different products in an effort to get back to the basics of competitiveness.

A more difficult case is that of American Express—the card company that says you should never leave home without it. Well, over the last couple of years, a lot of its cardholders have been lured away by the rash of new competitors. Recall that Entrenched organizations are particularly vulnerable to the entrance of new competitors, especially when customer tastes change. American Express has long been noted for superior service and pushed itself as the choice for discriminating cardholders at the upper end of the market. But as consumers began to desire gifts, gimmicks, discounts, and other amenities, card companies had to give them more than just service and image.

The solution is to diversify, either with respect to products or the base of customers. American Express is doing both. It's going after new types of customers. Look carefully the next time you're in a small strip malls, and you'll notice that this card is now being accepted in a class of business that American Express would never have let become merchants. In addition, it has developed new products. The Optima card is its attempt to provide a revolving-credit option, much like VISA and Master Card.

American Express's management has tried to improve the marketing of new products by touching base with all of their 50,000-plus employees in an effort to get everyone dancing to the same tune. Not that one should doubt their ability to pull it off, but the dichotomy of the Entrenched stage must be reckoned with. At American Express, the reins still tend to be held at the top without a lot of focus on the direct involvement of the workforce in generating ideas to alter the course of business. Second, the focus is still oriented toward the short term. We all have to pay the electric bill every month so there is a practical side to short-term thinking. But you must be willing to spend the time in order to get that ocean liner headed in another direction.

The Not-for-Profit Sector

Societal changes and economic woes have created tremendous obstacles for philanthropic and human services organizations. Many have slipped into the Entrenched stage because of outmoded strategies and a lack of attention to marketing. Nevertheless, there are numerous examples of not-for-profits that may be among the best-managed, innovative, and progressive organizational models around.

If you think it's tough to manage people who get paid to do what you need them to do, think how challenging it must be to have to motivate volunteers over whom you have hardly any authority but have a tremendous bearing and impact on the success of the organization. In 1989 Peter Drucker's article entitled "What Business Can Learn from Non-Profits" made reference to the Girl Scouts, an incredibly effective organization.[1] Girl Scouts employs a staff of something like 6,000 people nationwide but manages the efforts of over 730,000 volunteers. Another good example is the Salvation Army, which over the years has developed a competence in rehabilitating offenders, and doing it less expensively and better than anyone else. Its incredibly low recidivism rates (the percentage of offenders who end up back in prison) are nearly as unbelievable as the Girl Scouts' ability to manage its volunteer roster. Leadership, especially the ability to motivate and communicate, is a key feature of these organizations.

---

1. *Harvard Business Review* (July–August, 1989).

Managing vs. Leading

Definitions and Deficiencies

The most accurate definition of leadership may prove to be the most basic one. To lead implies a twofold responsibility: to teach and to set an example. There are a number of reasons that leading is such a difficult proposition, but the bottom line may be that these two responsibilities may be too much to expect from most people. The Entrenched organization may find itself with people who are willing to take on these responsibilities or who are able to handle them, but too often it is hard to find someone who is both willing and able. The result is a class of managers who cannot or do not function as leaders.

Additionally, employees are losing respect for managers. They may recognize that there are some good ones in their midst, but by and large the field of management and those who occupy that role have lost the respect of those they manage. The traditional, hierarchical approach to organizational structure often found in the Entrenched stage depends on respect and trust, and when those are absent, the outputs produced will lack the quality that it takes to be competitive in today's marketplace.

Government organizations tend to foster jaded public perceptions about the competence of their people, and nonprofits come under closer scrutiny, even to the point of having to justify their existence to those who support their causes. These outcomes are not the result of advances in technology or the success of the Japanese; they are the by-products of an insensitive management culture that has failed to calculate the movements of the stars and planets and is thus woefully off course in its attempts to get people to do the things they are paid to do at the level of quality that is needed.

You may have witnessed the reluctance of employees to seek promotion to supervisory or management positions. Many people simply do not want the daily headache associated with the job. They don't want to become one of the enemy and miss out on the chance to commiserate with their peers over lunch abut how little "they" care. This division between management and employees is not a new phenomenon, but the toxic levels of this infection have produced a type of gangrene in many organizations. And you know what happens next.

Someone must come along to restore respect for the authority that is invested in leadership. Without this, it is almost impossible for the Entrenched organization to seize opportunities.

Leadership and Communications

One of the several causes of the real or perceived lack of leadership is the age-old communications problem that every organization faces to some degree. Entrenched organizations just have it worse. Employees frequently feel left out of the loop, and in our CNN society, knowledge and information wield tremendous power. It isn't necessarily that those in positions of power and authority withhold information as much as they fail to keep people informed.

The reluctance to tell everyone that there is in fact no news gets misconstrued as an attempt to keep people in the dark. In other cases, the hesitancy of leaders to admit their mistakes is seen as another such concealment strategy. Most employees, staff people, volunteers, deacons, or administrative assistants know about your mistakes long before you ever even make them. Sometimes the pressure to maintain the proper image as leaders causes us to believe that mistakes are a sign of weakness, and the admission of error is seen as a loss of respect. It usually is the other way around. The failure to admit our shortcomings in the view of those who already are aware of them can nearly disqualify us from being seen as a leader. Sure, we'll maintain our stature as manager, division director, or whatever else, but the title of "someone we would be willing to follow" disappears in their minds.

The problem is that in the throes of organizational

change, information becomes an even more important commodity because it helps people to manage their emotional
reactions to an uncertain climate. If you've ever taken children
on a long car trip (or have listened to the lament of those who
have), the first thing you'll notice is that they have questions.
"Where are we going?" And "Are we there yet?" Now I'm not
proposing that the analogy of adults in an organization and
children on a long car trip is an exact one, but if you've been in
leadership any length of time, the point is clear.

Leadership and Mind-Sets

To manage change effectively, leaders must let others know
where they're going and keep them apprised of where they
are along the way. You've no doubt encountered the word
paradigm in the recent literature. A paradigm is simply a rule,
assumption, or principle to help us understand why things
work the way they do. Harmless as that may sound, these rules
can inhibit our ability to deal with change and to welcome new
ideas and ways of doing things.

The noted futurist Joel Barker in his training sessions on
the business of paradigms, cites the powerful example of the
Swiss watch industry whose world market share was dealt a
devastating blow by the upsurge of the liquid crystal diode
(LCD)–type timepieces. In fact, the Swiss themselves were the
creators of the LCD technology, but it did not fit the established
mind-sets for how a watch should operate. The idea was never
patented and was abandoned on display at a trade show where a
Japanese and an American businessman swooped it up and
made a fortune. The paradigm concept becomes real by this
example.

The point is not that LCD watches can match the crafts-
manship of the Swiss variety; it is that the idea that undid the
industry came from within the industry, but no one in it was
willing to recognize the opportunity presented by a new
technology. These so-called paradigm shifts can wreak havoc
on established mind-sets. This is a common dilemma at this
stage. Mind-sets can become so entrenched that not only do

we refuse to believe that the earth may be round but we even begin to doubt once again that it revolves around the sun. There may be a similar dynamic taking place in the culture of the Entrenched organization operating in today's workplace culture. We are undergoing a fundamental reevaluation of what we have always believed about leadership.

Playing Psychiatrist

Avoiding the Basics

Leadership is a straightforward subject that is made more complex by a tendency to avoid common sense, common courtesy, and common decency. Managers have been taught that they can figure out what people want rather than asking them. This tendency to play psychiatrist seemed to work for quite some time, but now the diagnoses are becoming far less accurate, and the patient seems to be more disturbed than ever before.

People want to be treated well. They have the same needs as leaders for real involvement, participation, and contribution, and they want to go home at the end of the workday knowing that the time spend yielded something of meaning and value. Over the years, there has been a subtle change in how people express those needs, and so leaders must adjust the application of common sense.

Whether it's because of unfulfilled promises or a reaction to environmental forces, it's apparent that the way we have been teaching people to manage and supervise has not taught them how to lead. Whether you're a branch chief in a government agency, executive director of an association, or chairman of the board, you probably have noticed that the theories and principles embraced twenty years ago seem to hold less valence.

Eliminating Management by Threat

Even in today's age of enlightenment, it's shocking that so many leaders still practice pressure tactics and dole out negative incentives by the truckload, believing they can force other people to produce. Certainly no one should be naive or too idealistic to think that fear doesn't have a role to play in motivating people in certain circumstances, but as a fundamental leadership style, it has nothing going for it.

Thomas Carlyle once said, "We must get rid of fear; we cannot act until then. A man's acts are slavish, not true but specious; his very thoughts are false, he thinks too as a slave and coward, till he has gotten fear under his feet." If you're a fan of Machiavelli, this may hit you as a bit soft, but today's environment is usually not a factory setting where people are expected to toe the line. In the Entrenched stage in particular we are asking them to think, to innovate, to create, to come up with ways to do more with less.

Providing the Information

Have you heard the story about involvement and commitment being illustrated by a plate of bacon and eggs? The chicken is involved, but the pig is committed. Whether you've heard it before or grin or grimace, there's an important point being made here. For people in today's organizational culture to support decisions actively and implement strategies, it makes sense to build their commitment.

At a component of the Defense Logistics Agency, the commanding general, colonels, and senior staff members were asked how many of them had noticed that their direct reports and their subordinates needed to have more questions answered before they gave their heartfelt buy-in? The unanimous show of hands reflected a phenomenon that is widespread though sometimes misunderstood. Followers do not want to do your job or to make your decisions. They simply need more information to assure them that the direction is sound. Like it or not, many leaders are in the driver's seat on that long trip.

You may be able to think of other paradigm shifts that are challenging our past practices in leadership. There exists no comprehensive assessment that captures it all. Whether it's

Tom Peters, Peter Senge, or W. Edwards Deming, we all have only a piece of a very important puzzle.

The Arnie Kleiner Story

Leadership Personified

Everyone has a favorite leadership example. Whether it's General Patton, Martin Luther King, Jr., or Eleanor Roosevelt, we see the skills and techniques of leadership once again embodied in the actions of men and women. By studying leaders, we believe we can unlock the secrets to success. This particular story is one of a leader who began in the worst of Entrenched situations. With the savvy of a world's greatest salesperson and the compassion of a rabbi, he was able not only to survive entrenchment but to revitalize an ailing television station and restore it to near dominance.

Back in 1983, Baltimore's WMAR-TV referred to itself as the "number four station in a three-station market." That should tell you all you need to know about the state of affairs in the organization and its self-perception. Its ratings and share of the local market were at an all-time low, and it had just lost its affiliation with the top national network. The broadcast equipment was old and wearing out due to a lack of any sort of preventive maintenance plan; internal procedures were inflexible to the point that something as simple as routing a call to the right department was a major accomplishment; the previous general manager had left behind an atmosphere saturated with fear and a staff of people who but for the need to pay the bills had all but given up; there were perpetual rumors about the station's being put on the market at a firesale price; and there were deep chasms between management and the three unions that represented the vast majority of the workforce. As if this wasn't enough, the day that Arnie took over as general manager, there was a near mob of picketers outside the building protesting the station's employment practices. Of course, this was the lead story on the evening news on all of the other channels in town.

Any way you looked at it, this was an Entrenched organization that had forgotten about strategy, cared little any longer about quality, and figured that since no one was watching its shows, there was no customer to get close to. To someone skilled in the field of management, this would be a nightmare situation. To a man or woman who feels born to lead, it's what getting up in the morning is all about. As this short story unfolds, you will notice many of the skills and techniques required at the Entrenched stage. What you cannot see are matters of the heart—determination, resolve, and will. These cannot be taught.

A Willing Ear

Unlike many other new chief executives, Arnie Kleiner's first act as general manager was not to issue edicts or commands or to utter slogans of encouragement. In fact he took no action at all. Instead he listened. He talked to employees, managers, consultants, community leaders . . . anyone he thought could shed some light on the next steps for WMAR.

He asked employees about the environment in the station. He wanted to hear what they had to say about the problems with their supervisors. He was interested in what they thought were strengths of the workplace that could be built upon. At first there was tremendous fear and threat, but gradually they began to see that he meant what he said. There was no retribution for speaking up and no one was labeled a malcontent, no matter how vitriolic his or her viewpoint might have been. Arnie knew people were hurting and wanted to give them a chance to vent their hostilities and begin to heal.

He asked his newly acquainted team of managers what teamwork had meant in the past and what it should mean in the future. He quizzed them about their ideas for revitalizing the news broadcast (the heart and soul of any local station), upgrading the technology, and establishing the station's community asset image (the primary emotional motivation for viewers to want to tune in). He also made it clear what his expectations of them would be (many were surprised): he wanted them to do their jobs and would give them the freedom to take risks. After all, what really did they have to lose?

He asked the experts in all quarters what needs were not being met and what other needs were out there that could be fulfilled. He brought technicians in to study the operation and give him the best overall picture of what was being done right and what was out of focus. By the time he had finished asking questions and listening to the responses, one thing was clear to everyone: this guy was different.

Putting the Pieces Back Together

Not everything he heard was pleasing. In fact there were some deep concerns over personnel matters, especially among top staff and even from those he reported to. An overbearing vice president of the company that owned WMAR was a continuous thorn in he flesh. He insisted that Arnie create "clear lines of responsibility and accountability." That wasn't such a bad idea, but the issue wasn't so much that people didn't know who was responsible and accountable; the problem was that no one wanted to assume either one in the face of a future that seemed impossible.

Ultimately a leader has to understand what motivates others and then put them in a position where they can reasonably expect to receive the rewards they desire. The tough part of a leader's job is dealing with personalities. Sometimes one or two people in key management positions can keep an Entrenched organization mired in quicksand because they refuse to cooperate with others.

Arnie faced that situation as well and through a series of group meetings determined who was willing to board the ship and set out for the New World and who had to be left behind. He hired new on-air talent, releasing others who were said to be untouchable under the old management regime. For those whose disposition and desires deemed them unfit to sail, he bid farewell. For those who were ready to set sail, he aligned their functions and reporting relationships. Rather than reorganize departments, he reorganized people, shifting them around to areas of challenge, new opportunity, or proven expertise. With an uneasy but hopeful crew, they pushed from the docks of their past practices and waited for the wind to direct them toward the future.

Putting Theory into Practice

It's one thing to be told that you'll get the chance to do things your way; it's another to have it happen to you. In the Entrenched stage, employees crave the opportunity to take control of their jobs but need a catalyst to accept the challenge. Arnie provided that catalyst at the department head level and saw to it that it was pushed all the way down the organization. For example, the news director was asked to develop a plan with his assistants and other key staffers to boost ratings and create a warm, friendly contact for viewers. The chief engineer had to take his staff through the same routine and come up with an approach to improving the on-air quality of all broadcasts. And so it went in each area, from sales to public affairs to programming.

There were lots of anxious moments in this process. On several occasions department heads were taken by surprise when the plans they submitted were actually followed up on. Some had apparently just gone through the motions, not believing that Arnie was serious about letting them do their jobs. The motto of department managers in the past had been, "Paid like a professional, treated like a child." They were not used to having the freedom to be creative and take risks or being accountable for the end results.

There was one crucial area in which Arnie's leadership skills may have been more responsible for turning things around than in any other: union negotiations. Past bargaining sessions were characterized by mistrust, hostility, and threats. Union representatives expressed their mistrust for the station's intentions and vocalized the hostilities they felt in being treated like replaceable parts rather than dedicated employees who wanted to feel pride in their performance. Station management's reply was to threaten to replace them with less expensive and less demanding technicians and talent. Neither side could see eye to eye.

Arnie recognized that union employees too could be freed up to take pride in their work and gave concessions in return for commitment. Management-union relationships are never problem free, but an unusual calm began to prevail within the workplace. It seemed as if workers dared to hope that things would actually improve. Arnie certainly was not perceived to be a saint, but he had won the trust of those whose trust was always the hardest to gain. While many climbed aboard with reluctance, expecting to get the chance to say "I told you so," there were no mutinies aboard ship.

A Lost Wallet and Morale

Perhaps the last-practiced leadership skills are the two dictionary definitions: to set an example and to teach. Most of us realize in the normal course of affairs that people pay correspondingly less attention to the spoken or written word in comparison with that which they observe. Memos go ceremonially unheeded, and verbal instructions become misconstrued, but actions are different. Leaders are under a microscope, and they must learn to live under close scrutiny. They are not permitted the same emotional excesses, tantrums, and pouting that their subordinates may indulge in. They must also consistently exhibit the behaviors that they want others to emulate.

After returning to his office from shooting a routine editorial, Arnie discovered that his wallet was missing. Television stations are a rough environment, and so he assumed that someone had pilfered it. With controlled but obvious anger, he sent a memo to all station staff announcing the theft but declaring amnesty for the perpetrator if he or she would just return the credit cards, driver's license, and other identification. Most of the staff was incensed at the thought that the general manager was accusing them. No one said anything, but the air was thick with hostility toward him on top of hurt feelings.

Three days after the incident, Arnie donned his studio jacket to do another editorial—and there was the wallet. One reaction would have been to put out the word sheepishly that the wallet had been found without alluding to details. Leaders, though, must see opportunity lurking in the shadows of every threat. Arnie decided to send out another memo letting everyone know that he had blown it and that for the rest of the day everyone could "feel free to call me a you-know-what to my face instead of behind my back like you usually do." For the entire day, everyone from the janitor to the weatherman made it a point to take him up on his offer. From that moment forward, there was a noticeable change in the morale of WMAR-TV; making a mistake was no longer the end of the world.

There are a lot of other stories of this same nature illustrating how Arnie's skills helped to create an environment in which innovation replaced frustration and the challenge of a New World replaced the monotony of a hopeless future. Not only did the station's ratings and share turn around, but WMAR made a serious run at becoming the number one station in Baltimore, and it won numerous national awards for its creative programming and community efforts. Perhaps the greatest testimony to the success story was that the station became a hot property in the broadcast market and was bought and sold several times during Arnie's tenure, always at a substantial profit and always with the condition that he stay on as general manager.

Leadership Skills

While it is impossible to reproduce the character and personality of a leader such as Arnie Kleiner, the skills that can create change in the Entrenched stage are easily documented. Four

are particularly valuable: supportive communications, alignment of tasks and people, empowerment of the organization,
and raising expectations.

Supportive Communications

The quality of communications depends as much on the
climate that is created as on the words that are used. When it
becomes clear that the boss isn't really interested in your ideas,
it's demoralizing. Moreover, it has a chilling effect on your
desire to be creative or to think through thorny problems and
tackle tough issues. Its deenergizing when the boss's communications approach puts you on the defensive. You spend
more time coming up with a rebuttal than actually communicating. The way to energize people is to show empathy for
their concerns and to establish a dialogue based on problem
solving. Arnie's managers frequently left meetings having
agreed to doing it his way but feeling good about it. They
knew they had been heard and that the outcome was based on
what was best for the station, and not the whim of the person
in charge.

Alignment of Tasks and People

In the Entrenched stage, it is hard to produce results if there is
a high level of burn-out. Over time the wrong people end up
in the wrong jobs—managers who don't have people skills,
supervisors who lack technical expertise, and line workers
who never obtained the proper training. Leadership must
intervene and create the best alignment of people and tasks.
Sometimes this means making major changes in job descriptions or even demoting people who don't have the skills to
function effectively where they are currently. Often this
action is welcome; no one really likes to fail, but also no one is
likely to come forward and let it be known that he or she is out
of place. There is also an added benefit to moving people
around in that renewed enthusiasm can spring forth.

Empowerment of the Organization

One of the best-kept secrets of the American workplace is that the person doing the job has more insight than anyone else. We seem to believe that the person managing or supervising the person who does the job knows more. With that attitude, you'll never get an employee in an Entrenched organization to innovate. Empowerment simply means turning over more authority to employees for figuring out how their function can contribute to the overall goals of the organization. It isn't a complicated concept at all. The problem is that managers seldom want to relinquish authority. That's one reason their attempts at delegation are so unsuccessful. They give the person extra work and responsibility without the authority to do it right. The experience of empowered organizations is uniformly positive. Given more of an opportunity to control their destiny, employees will tend to outperform the standards that managers would have set for them.

Raising of Expectations

There is a well-known principle in behavioral science referred to as the Pygmalion principle, after the title of George Bernard Shaw's play. It seems that people will perform to whatever level you expect them to, no matter how high or low. For example, if a grade school teacher tells a student that she is an outstanding writer, the child will tend to excel beyond her normal ability. If the teacher tells the same child that she is slow in mathematics, then the student will consistently perform much lower than her aptitude would merit. In the Entrenched stage it is common for organizational expectations to have deteriorated significantly. WMAR-TV had some real problems but mainly it was doing so poorly because no one expected anything more. Once those expectations were raised, it was easy to make progress.

For the most part, the Entrenched stage does present far more threat than opportunity. Just about every organization will find itself here at some point, usually the result of what wasn't done—the actions that were not taken or the warnings that were not heeded. For many, it is a wasteland of lost youth as the organization has allowed itself to slip into a catatonia of sorts or, worse, to have become rife with cynicism and apathy. This is a time of reckoning on the future of the organization; often the ability to thrive once again, or to blunder ahead listlessly, may depend on the personality, style, strength, and energy of leadership.

Eight

Recreating in The Complex Stage: The Culture of the Game

There are three things for which there is no solution: inflation, dandruff, and bureaucracy.

Malcolm Forbes, publisher

The last stage of organizational change that we'll discuss is the Complex stage. If there was a synonym for it, it would be "bureaucratized" or something to that effect. At this point an organization faces the toughest of choices: recreate itself or slowly self-destruct. Here we will find a culminating lesson in dealing with change, bringing forward many of the ideas that have been applied in previous stages.

The term *Complex* refers not so much to the sophistication of the work systems and processes of an organization but to the layers of rules and procedures that get in the way of the work. In this manner the problems are an order of magnitude worse than those of any other stage. It is described as the Culture of the Game. The priority in the workplace leans more to paying homage to a set of unwritten rules about how power and influence are distributed than paying attention to productivity, efficiency, or service to the customer.

If there is any one factor that accounts for an organization's slipping into Complexity, it is the lack of leadership exhibited in the Entrenched stage. The failure to make decisions, to share information, and to create involvement and participation becomes the way of life throughout the structure. The apathy and cynicism that become apparent in any poorly functioning entity escalate in the Complex stage to hidden agendas and politics. These now dominate the actions of individuals. I'm not talking about a lack of ethics or morals; it's more like a contagious disease, and once people are infected, little can be done to hide its symptoms.

Characteristics of the Game

It doesn't seem coincidental that many people refer to succeeding in their careers as "learning to play the game." This can represent a wide range of actions that are apart from the real purposes of the organization. For example, satisfying the demands of the hierarchy and learning to curry favor from the higher-ups can become more important than producing results in line with the mission. It becomes a system of management by whim rather than by objectives.

If you consider the characteristics of any sort of game you may observe a number of striking similarities to the environment of the Complex organization. In a game:

1. There must be a winner and a loser.
2. Keeping score is important.
3. You choose sides in order to play.
4. You learn to play well through practice.
5. Personal statistics are recorded regardless of what happens to the team.
6. There may be cheerleaders who instigate from the sidelines.
7. Referees are needed to maintain order.

The Culture of the Game creates a setting whereby power becomes the object of everyone's affections. Learning where the power lies, who has, how to get it, or how to protect yourself from it occupy the attention of employees at all levels. The rules of the game are frequently changed to serve the needs of those in power and to make it more difficult for newcomers to fit in. In fact, it is as if the rules begin to govern much of what takes places.

A Word about Government

When we get to this stage, we can't help but think of government institutions because of their age, size, and, unfortunately, their reputation, but these concepts apply to a lot of other kinds of entities as well. The knock against government managers' being "incompetent" is unfair, to say the least. I'm not saying these organizations don't have their share of deadwood and they don't suffer from some severe image problems, but so do a lot of others. In fact, it may take more skill to be good in the public sector. Let me explain.

You can find incompetence everywhere, but in government the constraints tend to make theirs more visible. When an organization is making a profit in the private sector, the general public assumes it is doing a good job and management is capable. It's inconceivable to the average person that the organization could take in billions of dollars otherwise. Well, there are lots of companies that do exactly that. Here are some empirical data. In *In Search of Excellence*, Tom Peters and Bob Waterman identified a long list of "excellent" companies; some eighteen months later a bunch of them were either in Chapter 11 bankruptcy or had closed up shop altogether.[1] Management experts analyzed their plight as deterioration in the quality of management.

If we looked inside these organizations, we would find that poor management had been the norm, but like a cancer it didn't show up as long as the patient was active and feeling

---

1. (New York: Warner Books, 1982).

good. The message here is that as long as an organization in the private sector is making a buck or two, no one really looks at the quality of management. Government managers have no such camouflage for their incompetencies. They struggle under mission statements that don't *narrow* their focus on whom they will serve and how but actually are written to be intentionally broad, mandating that they serve just about all the "customers" out there, no matter how unrealistic that may actually be.

If a private company realizes it is too expensive or impractical to serve a particular customer segment, of course, it can opt to move out of that particular line of business or type of customer. With only rare exception is that possible with public organizations. As a matter of fact, just let them get good at something (like the Social Security Administration's prowess in technology), and they get to carry out the programs that other agencies can't handle. This extra work ultimately stretches their capabilities to the breaking point.

Also observe how ex–civil servants go into business for themselves and make a bundle and how hotshot corporate types get appointments to run federal agencies and burn out in six months. Suffice it to say that to be good in the public sector may take more agility, flexibility, and persistence than anywhere else. The bottom line is that government, based on our historic paradigm, has been insulated from the factors that make Complexity a deadly disease, as it is in the private sector. One would have never expected this to change but it is. Today, even government can go out of business.

The Human Factor

The most telling result of the bureaucratic environment is that it destroys the value of human contact and human judgment. The buck is passed and never stops. When we turn our emphasis away from issues and toward policies, we slowly erode our ability to think. If we aren't getting good performance or if someone will not adhere to the rules of the culture, we create a policy that punishes everyone. It is said of bureaucracy that we will shoot nine innocent people just to get the tenth person who actually committed the crime.

At the same time, the necessity of interacting and collaborating with diverse groups of *people* diminishes. The inability to deal with people who are different destroys openness. There is tremendous fear in confronting others whose behavior we don't understand or which doesn't fit with how the game is supposed to be played. When the human contact quotient becomes low enough, unspoken conflicts erupt—conflict between departments, between levels and functions, between genders, between ethnic groups. All are given labels as expressions of our frustration. Like the addicted gambler, we know that the game is not good for us, but we just can't seem to stop playing.

How Opposites Attract

The Nature of Differences

In order for the Complex organization to recreate itself, it must bring those unspoken conflicts to the surface and dismantle the barriers between the players in the game. This may entail looking behind the labels that have been created. For example, counterpoised terms like *manager* and *worker* speak of an almost unconscious categorizing of people based on some concept of their relative value. After all, aren't "managers" supposed to be "workers" too? While you may object to reading this much into the terms, semantics can say a great deal about the nature of the problem.

Our tendency to deal only with the obvious areas of difference masks some of the deeper issues in the workplace. There is no question that our handling of gender, ethnic, and racial issues is inadequate. While we know the right things to say and in some cases have recruited the right numbers of various groups of people, there are still significant barriers to their full acceptance into the culture of the organization. If you study the demographic projections for the workplace, you will notice that it will become even more diverse, to the point that the term *minority* will have little meaning. Unless organizations embrace the contributions that diversity can offer, they are in for far more conflict than ever before.

This is a critical issue for the Complex organization. For example, if you look at how organizations have dealt with gender issues, and in particular the subject of sexual harassment, it seems that they may have missed the mark entirely. Policies have been implemented that are supposed to prevent harassment. Because the average person lacks a real understanding of the nature of gender differences from a cultural standpoint (not to mention the fact that the policies themselves, are unclear), the easiest way to stay out of trouble is to avoid contact in the first place. This solution, though, seriously undermines productivity and may create more exclusion on a gender basis rather than help to eliminate barriers.

Fundamental Differences between Individuals

Perhaps one of the greatest contributions in appreciating the value of differences has been the work of Isabel Briggs Myers and Katharine C. Briggs, a mother-daughter team of social scientists. The Myers-Briggs Type Indicator has been used to help managers understand various modes of expression. The theory is that it is very difficult to know how to deal with other people without understanding yourself first. The assessment reveals the strength of individual preferences for dimensions of personality, such as how you interact with others, how you process information, how you deal with facts and emotions, or how you deal with the concept of time. It can also be used to analyze temperaments, indicating whether you are more of a visionary, a stabilizing force, a problem solver, or a "people" person.

The point is this: even when we deal with individuals who seem to be the same, there are innate differences that need to be understood. Without this knowledge, the tendency is to suppress conflict. In the Complex stage, conflict between people is something to be avoided because it reminds us of the more glaring inconsistencies that the Culture of the Game spawns. The emotional scars that are inflicted through rejection and isolation sometimes never heal.

The Importance of Education

We should be educating ourselves to how differences can create a synergistic effect in the workplace that improves decision making, planning, and problem solving. In fact, opposites really do attract, and they provide a balance that is not available when the focus is on sameness. No one person can see the complete picture, and the tendency in the Complex organization is to stifle any expression that does not match the status quo. Unfortunately, it is the status quo that got us into trouble in the first place.

One of the reasons that approaches like quality management tend to fail in the Complex stage is that they hinge on the collective effort to pinpoint problems. Up and down the organizational structure, the motivations are to the contrary. Upper management has learned almost to look down on the lower-level employees regardless of how long they've been around. Field personnel have learned to be distrustful of headquarters staff. They feel as if "headquarters people" don't do much to earn their salaries except make up more rules. We have created multiple cultures in the workplace, over and beyond the more obvious ones that exist. There is as much animosity, stereotyping, and prejudicial behavior among various functional groups as there is between ethnic groups, races, genders, or generations.

If you were being transferred to a foreign country, you probably would invest some time in learning a little bit about the language, customs, and manners. More than likely, you would be sensitive to the potential for misunderstanding based on differences in culture. That same approach in the workplace would do a world of good. Some Complex organizations treat their departments and work units like foreign countries. But when you are playing a game, taking the time to understand people is low on the list of priorities.

The Real Truth about Teamwork

What Is a Team Player?

One of the automatic responses of management in the Complex stage is to try to create a synergistic effect but without dealing with the core issues. We have fostered and promoted severe division between levels and between departments that makes teamwork nearly impossible.

One problem is that the definition of "team player" based on the sameness philosophy is a barrier. Suppose you are in a staff meeting and the boss throws out an idea for consideration or even to gauge the reactions and thought process of the management team. In the Emerging or Expanding phase, there are likely to be some candid responses, disagreements and perhaps even controversial statements around the table. There will be greater interest in testing the validity of the idea than saying what the boss wants to hear. In the Complex stage this same scenario might play out quite differently. Those seated around the table will feel a strong pressure to support the idea, all the while believing that it's not a good one. There will be a sense of guilt as each gives in to the party line but an even greater sense that the risk of speaking up is too great. Sadly, their fears are often justified. In these cases, even those brave souls who do have the courage to speak up are quickly labeled as rebels, dissidents, or malcontents.

In the Complex stage a team player will be defined as one who avoids rocking the boat rather than one who does what is best for the team. In reality, it may be that the most dangerous people are the ones who never say anything. It may be that the people who don't care don't complain either. It may be that the passionate outburst of the so-called troublemaker is a warning cry from someone who cares very deeply about whether the organization succeeds or fails. When we make capitulation the price of team membership, we are essentially shooting ourselves in the foot—or worse.

The Bureaucratic Breakdown

Team efforts are also poisoned when the interaction styles of people in the organization follow the pattern of bureaucracy itself. In other words people play games with each other. Sometimes there is a lack of skill, other times a lack of integrity. But in either case manipulation, coercion, and political maneuvering are tactics that undermine any hope of creating a productive climate.

The use of these tactics stems from the approach to management that often accompanies this stage. The Complex organization relies on a sophisticated hierarchy to act as the governing force of norms, behaviors, and guidelines of the workplace culture. This hierarchical structure tends to be oppressive in its style, with top managers seen more as "fathers" and "mothers" rather than as people with higher-order responsibilities. Often this scenario resembles the operation of an abusive and dysfunctional family.

The parent relies on compliance and the enforcing of rules to motivate employees. There is a decidedly "because-I-told-you-so-that's-why" reply to questions and inquiries from staff members and subordinates. Punishment is preferred over positive reinforcement. Empathy for the emotional needs of workers is altogether absent as the parent seldom sees the legitimacy of any request for additional resources or the like. Among themselves, the parents seek to undermine each others' standing in the eyes of the children and position themselves to pass the blame for failures to someone else. Open abuse may be rare; subtle innuendos, indirect assaults, and veiled threats serve essentially the same purpose.

In the presence of the parent(s) employees exhibit an attitude of deference and respect (fear) but once out of their sight the talk turns quickly to the baser aspects of organizational life. An underground rebellion in the hearts of people makes it difficult for even the most dedicated of workers to avoid the temptation of sabotaging plans and programs. This sabotage is typically neither overt nor particularly unethical in the moral sense. It takes the form of doing slightly less than one is capable of, without actually violating the precise tenets of the job description. Important details don't get passed along. Asking for additional assignments is totally out of the question and may even engender hostility from co-workers. All of these are much like an unhappy teenager in a dysfunctional setting who does a halfway job of cleaning his or her room, neglects to relay important telephone messages, or avoids eating with everyone else at the dinner table.

In an abusive and dysfunctional family setting, members are obviously incapable of operating as a team. In fact their sole attention is on strategizing ways to avoid the possibility of abuse or how to come out the winner in the conflicts that occur. The games that are played are emotionally draining and imprint hopelessness on the psyches of members. Even sincere attempts at change are greeted with searing skepticism. This is why strategic planning, total quality, or customer service has little chance of being perceived as anything other than a fad in the Complex stage. People's expectations have been raised too often only to come crashing down. One can take but so much disappointment.

The Competitive Factor

The last element that undermines teamwork is the impact of competition. This is a tough issue to broach because of our emphasis as a culture on the virtues of competitiveness. We educate our children very early on the importance of getting ahead, urging them to acquire the right experiences and exposure. We pay homage to sports figures who give many of us the vicarious thrill of competing as they play out all of life's passion in a few hours or less.

In the Emerging stage, competition is one of the keys to internal productivity and external success. But actions must coincide with the dynamics of the stage of change that the organization finds itself in, and competition offers little help in the Complex stage.

The reason is simple. The bureaucratic (parental) mentality of the Complex stage makes competition a destructive element. The fear of failure outweighs the potential for success. People compete against each other rather than against some standard of excellence. When functions are pitted against each other, under the premise that competition will improve the end product, things often disintegrate quickly. The lack of positive reinforcement makes competition appear as a gladiatorial contest—even the winner must perish eventually.

What is needed to salvage any vestige of teamwork is collaboration. Leaders who have the courage to go against the grain of manipulative tactics may find it possible to install a reward system that motivates employees to work together. This is essential because there is no other way out of the Complex stage.

Creating the Right Climate: "Crazy Joe" And The Charlottesville Public Schools

Background

Crazy Joe may not sound like a term of endearment but it is. Dr. Joseph McGeehan, superintendent of the Charlottesville public schools, received this unlikely moniker for his elegant handling of an organization in the Complex stage. Despite his calm personality and the genteel nature of a former Benedictine monk, he jarred the school division out of its catatonia and enabled it to face reality. He was able to establish a climate where school officials, teachers, parents, business and community leaders, and the students themselves all came together to share their insights about how to make that reality work for everyone involved.

Charlottesville was an ideal school division in many ways. Being situated in a small but sophisticated university town and having an enrollment of only 4500, one would think that there could be few serious problems. But subtly the demographics of the population had begun to shift. The number of students from disadvantaged backgrounds had increased substantially, as had ethnic, racial, and religious diversity. Money for education had always been plentiful in the past, but more recently the pursestrings had tightened, forcing some difficult choices for the school board. As in many other communities across the country, substance abuse, crime, and teen pregnancy had also found their way into the classrooms and hallways.

Not only was this community not prepared to cope with these issues, but there was a denial that would not even allow them to admit that their heralded school system was under attack. Statistics on student performance were not released for fear of the community's becoming enraged, and there was little discussion over how to bridge gaps in class and race. A group of vigilant parents had actually forced the creation of a new middle school that would prevent their children from having to mix with others whom these parents believed were lowering the standards. In the community, there was a storm raging over what kind of school system Charlottesville should be. The expectations of parents and the capability of the schools were miles apart. What was demanded could not be delivered.

The superintendents who preceded Dr. McGeehan had apparently chosen to ignore these problems in hopes that they might disappear. But as we all know, problems generally do not go away; they just get worse. It had gotten to the point now that administrators were doing whatever was the safest, the easiest, or whatever would keep them off the front pages of the local paper. Everyone still cared passionately about the children and about professionalism, but the fog of the Complex stage had rolled in, blurring the sense of purpose and urgency.

Enter the Dragon

Dr. McGeehan had served as deputy superintendent for the Kansas City Public Schools. He was no stranger to change or

the controversy that accompanies progress, having adminis-
tered school desegregation in the late 1960s. He was an ardent
student of education itself, well read, and conversant in the
latest research on approaches to learning. As well, he was an
outstanding manager, negotiator, and writer. But none of
these characteristics could account for his ability to revitalize a
Complex organization. What was it then?

"Crazy Joe" did not care what people thought. Yes, he
understood the political environment and worked extremely
well with a talented but cautious school board. Sure, he could
appreciate the fragile predicament of his assistant superintendents and their being gunshy about change. He was in touch
with the mind-set of principals, curriculum coordinators, and
classroom teachers. And no question about it, he sympathized
with parents in all of the diverse communities in their quest
for a quality education for their children. But still, he didn't
care what they thought.

He simply knew what it would take for Charlottesville
public schools to avoid disaster and was willing to do what it
took to get out of the game. He was neither insensitive nor
dogmatic, but there was a stern resolve that made it impossible
for people to be neutral about how they felt about him. The
more he talked to people, the more it was obvious that he was
right. He was willing to risk being run out of town on a rail
in order to convince the public to see things the way they
were and to work together for them to become the way they
should be.

The specific actions he took are less important than the
objectives that guided those actions. In essence he created a
climate that made it possible and safe for school personnel and
the public to consider what type of school division they really
needed. He made it possible for a cross-section of business and
community leaders to shed insights on the demands of the
twenty-first century and what type of product should be
developed by the schools. He made it possible for the school
board to establish a rapport with the school personnel that
allowed each to appreciate the contributions and talent of the
other. If you are at all familiar with the dynamics of public

education, you will recognize that these are major accomplishments.

"Crazy Joe" did the only thing you can do in the Complex stage: he recreated the foundation on which the school division was built. In this stage of change, it is impossible to deal with the future by simply doing what you have done better, or faster, or longer, or improving its quality. The only possible solution to Complexity is to start over. This will never happen until the organization faces the fact that it can no longer proceed with the same set of assumptions that it has in the past. Until it realizes that its viability is based on near-revolutionary change, its chances are never good.

Principles of Recreation

Recreating is different from resurrection, when something is brought back to life. The Charlottesville Public Schools, like any other Complex organization, was faced not with death but extinction. The notion that entities like government or public schools can go out of business is still a bit farfetched, but it is definitely more likely than it was a decade ago. Complexity is not just counterproductive; it is destructive because the actions of the organization amplify the problems of those who are being served *and* those who perform the work. This is a tremendous waste of resources in any environment. In the austerity we are faced with today, it is also criminal.

There are a lot of enlightened leaders who are at the helm of Complex organizations, struggling to reverse the trend and establish a new direction or focusing on creating a new purpose. It is from the latter school of thought that the following principles originate.

1. *Examine the historical assumptions on which the organization has been based.* In public education, children no longer work on the farm, yet they still have a summer vacation (so they could help with the harvest) and end each day at 3:00 P.M. (so they could make the long walk home before it got dark). In

the Complex stage, these assumptions must be challenged and replaced. Dr. McGeehan motivated stakeholders to create new assumptions and belief systems. Unless this happens, no one will be willing or able to exercise the ingenuity to solve the problems of the future.

2. *Sell the long-term perspective.* It has been said a million times but not yet been heard in the majority of Complex organizations: it has taken a long time to get into a mess, and it will take some time to get out of it. The idea is not to suggest that it has to take a long time at all—in fact, recreation can take place in two or three years—but to shift the basis of incentives and expectations and give a new set of assumptions the opportunity to take root. If public opinion, employee incentives, and political horizons can be stretched beyond the immediate present, there is a good chance for success.

3. *Develop and champion a model to describe the recreated state.* In the Entrenched stage, we needed leadership. Now we need a champion—an individual (or a group of them) with personal courage and unflinching resolve. The role of the champion is to develop a model of the recreated organization that shows what it should be doing and what it should look like. This is beyond the scope of strategic planning, although the elements may be similar. A strategic plan outlines objectives and actions based on known key factors for success. Here, the Complex organization recreates those key factors and generates a new culture, philosophy, and rules.

4. *Organize a broad constituency for recreation.* Dr. McGeehan called them "planning teams." They were simply groups of diverse constituencies who cared about the quality of education. He sent out surveys to a good portion of the 40,000 residents of Charlottesville; held meetings in the public housing sections of the city and motivated residents to go door to door to canvas those who were not in attendance; gathered parents and teachers together to talk openly about their needs and frustrations; appeared on talk shows and radio programs and invited the press to be a part of what was taking place; and called on religious leaders to preach the message from their

pulpits. By the time these groups had finished, two things were clear: there was much more consensus than anyone ever imagined, and there were plenty of concrete ideas to recreate with.

5. *Establish and monitor benchmarks and timetables.* A new set of assumptions and key factors for success provides a new basis by which to measure success. This is a major need for the Complex organization. The Culture of the Game promotes unrealistic or irrelevant performance standards and ignores the evaluation of outcomes. Recreation allows you to establish the outcomes that will measure what you need to be doing as opposed to what you have always done. In Charlottesville, new measures of student potential began to replace measures of student performance. With a new assumption that the purpose of education was to create life-long learning, what students do five years from now becomes more critical than what they did last semester. Monitoring and reporting on these benchmarks helps employees and stakeholders make it to the long term. As long as people know that progress is being made, they will have the patience necessary to allow a recreation. In the Complex stage we get used to keeping everyone in the dark, and they quickly lose confidence even if things are actually getting better.

Postscript

When a Complex organization is recreated, what stage does it go to? Dr. McGeehan is still in the process of recreating the Charlottesville Public Schools, but the foundation has been laid and is being built upon. It has moved across the change cycle and reentered the Emerging stage. The school population is somewhat stable, and other conditions make expansion unlikely in the near term. While this is common, it is by no means the rule. The conditions in the external environment can also cause recreation to place the organization in the Expanding stage or even in Maturity. In that event, the prescriptions for those stages can be applied, and so the cycle continues. In Charlottesville, with "Crazy Joe" at the helm, no one will fall asleep at the wheel any time soon.

Nine

When the Rubber Meets the Road: How to Manage Change

You don't get the breaks unless you play with the team instead of against it.

Lou Gehrig, *major league baseball player*

If we could imagine the ideal culture for an organization, it would be that of an Orchestra, with the diversity of the instruments coupled with their ability to make a harmonious sound. Each instrument is important in its own right, for without it the sound would be incomplete. But all of the musicians know that no individual can take the credit since success is based on the fusion of their respective parts. The elements of practice and planning make an obvious analogy to the workplace, as is the focus on pleasing the customer, the audience.

The Conductor of the orchestra performs many of the same leadership roles that are needed in any organization. He or she interprets the piece of music to get a sense of how it should be played and then communicates this vision to the musicians. They work together to make adjustments between the vision and what is possible given the talent (resources) of the group. The Conductor's job is to balance the needs of highly professional individuals with the goal of having them sound as if only one person is playing. The Conductor is also very careful about making too many changes, especially at the last minute, for fear of disrupting the gentle balance of the group.

We have covered most of the bases in dealing with change from an organizational perspective and need to wrap up by considering the impact of change on individuals. With insight into handling the natural resistance, you can become a champion of change. Rather than simply knowing how to deal with change when you are confronted with it, you will be able to seek it and embrace it.

This is not a prescription for change for its own sake. It is the recognition that change is the one thing we can depend on. Much is said about the need to be "proactive." In most instances, this is an overrated concept. Most of life is reactive, and so it is unreasonable to pressure managers to develop their sixth senses, but it is necessary to narrow that gap between the time change hits and the response. If you recall the discussion of latent change, it is this same mind-set that we need to apply in dealing with people.

Digging in Their Heels

Change vs. Variety

Human beings have an amazing capacity when it comes to change. We are able to absorb the impact to such a degree that the untrained eye would not even know we were experiencing any reaction at all. On the other hand, those of us who do the changing sometimes forget what it feels like to go through it.

We are somewhat put off by the reluctance of others to buy into our strategies and plans. We are uncomfortable when the resistance comes to the surface, and the others dig their heels in and refuse to budge. For these reasons, it is useful to explore the finer points of the human response.

One of the theories on human behavior is that people actually like change. A new set of job responsibilities or a change in scenery is seen as positive for the average person. Much of the empirical evidence, however, seems to suggest just the opposite. Ask a roomful of people how many of them would like a three-week-all-expenses-paid vacation to the south of France. How many would go for it? You're right; probably everyone. If you then asked how many would consider moving to Marseille, what might the response be? Sure, there's always one or two in every group, but for the most part, few would be willing to relocate permanently. Finally, how many, after enjoying three weeks of sand, sun, and fun, would return home, plop down on the couch in the indented spot where they always sit, and say to themselves, "Gee, it's good to be back home"?

What we discover here is that people like variety much more than change. Change is unsettling, no matter what the circumstances. Even positive change has a price tag on it. A huge promotion, for example, would be a nice thing to have happen, but it would still involve a series of emotional adjustments. It is the ability to analyze these adjustments that gives managers the tools to lead people through change.

Maintaining Homeostasis

A basic principle of biology is that a living being will tend toward an internal balance (or equilibrium) by adjusting its external surroundings. Herein lies one of the key issues in managing the human side of change: the fight for balance is the source of resistance, and it will surface in every situation to varying degrees. In fact, the concept of homeostasis helps explain both mental and emotional responses to change.

Anything that is not perceived to be consistent with the normative state of affairs will face severe opposition.

The human brain itself performs this function for us on a continuous basis. Our sensory perceptions work to exclude new information from becoming part of the neurological response. In other words, the brain screens out anything that doesn't contribute to its known conditions for survival. People who are judged to be incapable of functioning in society are often those who lack the ability to carry out this operation. Their brains fail to screen out information, and so they do whatever the foreign stimulus suggests.

In an organizational setting, each person strives to find and to hang on to his or her own homeostasis. While people may complain about the routine and the sameness of what they do, just try changing it in a way that creates an unfamiliar environment. Resistance will surface in short order. There are a number of different kinds of homeostatic factors that change can disrupt. Often the complaints about a particular decision or plan that is being implemented can be traced back to those factors, even though the surface issues seem focused on other aspects of the situation.

For example, the consolidation of two research facilities requires that a group of scientists relocate. You may hear them voice complaints about how the move will be detrimental to the future of their projects, when actually it is their personal and family schedules that have been disrupted by the move. Homeostatic factors fall into several categories:

• *Functional responsibilities*. This is the need for stability and predictability in routine tasks and job dimensions. In the Emerging stage, we talked about the value of strategic planning and how structural changes could be necessary to make the most of market opportunities. In the Expanding stage, we discussed the redesign of systems and procedures. Whenever these kinds of adjustments are made, they can benefit the organization but wreak havoc on employees. Even a positive alteration in functional roles can create resistance. Whenever position descriptions are rewritten or performance standards negotiated in the midst of change, employees will either bargain to accomplish more than is being required or less than is desired. An astute manager will keep standards within a range that is high enough to challenge the employee but low enough that achieving them is possible.

- *Skill levels.* Often change can create a setting in which employees must acquire new or better skills within the same job function. This is unsettling because it requires major adjustments in dealing with personal confidence. You may have experienced the introduction of a new technology such as word processing where this factor was present. For years clerical employees may have complained about having to use typewriters while the rest of the world has gone to computers. Once people realize that learning DOS is not like a QWERTY keyboard they begin to complain once again that productivity is going down because of wasted time on the computer. In fact, what may be at issue is the transition to a new skill level.

- *Work habits.* People develop a comfort level in dealing with their coworkers that change can disrupt. This would also include changes in the degree of interaction with those outside the organization. Resistance will take the form of concerns for productivity and efficiency, while in truth the issue is the imbalance created by having to adjust personal styles and communications approaches. The use of teaming as a way of improving interdepartmental relationships is a common strategy that can produce this effect. Another common change situation occurs when travel is either added or taken away, depending on the life-style preferences of the individual.

- *Span of control.* This factor is similar to work habits except that it deals with the stability created through responsibilities in management, supervision, and other authority structures. Any change in this area can create an imbalance in the power perception of the individual as well as in that person's sense of value to the organization.

- *Reporting relationships.* Stability in reporting relationships can be a vital element in job satisfaction. In fact, quality of supervision is one of the primary sources of employee motivation. Sometimes even a mediocre supervisor is better than a new one because of the unknowns.

▪ *Space*. Stability in surroundings is more a matter of the degree of privacy that the individual is accustomed to maintaining. Again, change can work either way. Designing office systems when people are used to working behind closed doors can be just as disruptive as installing cubicles when employees are used to being in plain sight of each other.

▪ *Time*. People like to maintain some stability in their schedules. Recently organizations have gone to flextime, working ten hours a day and getting every other Friday off, and the like. Ordinarily a more advantageous work schedule will not affect homeostasis unless it results in a less advantageous personal schedule, such as one that would interfere with family or social activities.

▪ *Commitment levels*. People develop a level of caring and concern for what happens in the workplace. Some prefer being able to detach themselves from the job. Others thrive on being emotionally engaged with the organization and prefer to stay connected. Change may require more commitment than some are willing to give, and restructuring of the operation could distance others from being in touch with what's happening.

The common theme is that people have varying needs for stability even around the same homeostatic factor. Only through open communication and interaction with employees can a manager really know from which direction resistance will come. The only assurance is in knowing that it will certainly come. Not only is there variety of resistance to change, but individuals also play different roles when change is being implemented.

Roles and Influence

Knowledge of those roles is crucial in dealing with resistance. In fact, it is vital to the leader's role as well since a lot of change is externally generated, and many of us are called on to implement someone else's plan. Each role will also produce a unique set of challenges in commitment building. Depending on the kind of change being implemented, you may find yourself playing multiple roles, either in reality or based on the perceptions of those around you. Here is a look at the various roles:

- *Initiator.* This is the person who is responsible for the change itself. His or her interest in the outcome of the implementation will be in terms of how it satisfies the objectives. The initiator will frequently be an external party and may even be one who has no real appreciation for constraints in the organization. This happens a lot in government when legislators enact changes that affect the operations of an agency in ways that run counter to what agency employees believe makes sense. In the Expanding stage, this becomes less of an issue because the emphasis is placed on getting external parties involved in the operations as a way of doing business.

- *Facilitator.* The facilitator role is played by those who are tasked with the actual implementation of change. They perhaps have the most difficult job because they must rally support for ideas that they may not consent to. Their options are to deal openly with their feelings, pretend that they are supportive, or make the organization (or initiator) the common enemy. The long-term benefits are on the side of openness. Facilitators must get in touch with their real feelings about the change, educate themselves on the parameters of the change, and develop a strategy to communicate to others without damaging their enthusiasm or raising unnecessary tensions.

- *Benefactors.* Organizational development consultants Michael Doran and Priscilla Bell Cuddy, of Legacy Management Associates are noted experts in the field of change management in the government. In their work with agencies like the Department of Energy, they note how benefactors are actually the ones to whom the arrow of change is aimed. More often than not, they are disrupted by change even though upper levels of management may perceive that the change is "good" for them or for the functions that they perform. Here is where the strongest resistance will come from. The best response is to concentrate on information sharing and keep the communications channels open. We'll continually come across this role in discussing the emotional needs of employees.

- *Gatekeeper.* There will normally be an individual or a group of them whose resistance to a particular change is centered on their estimation of the feasibility of the proposed implementation. If they are left out of the front end of the process, they have no recourse but to oppose any intentions. The problem is that once it gets to this point, they will resist the idea as well as the way it is intended to be done. Often the idea is acceptable to them, but from their vantage point the way it's being done is flawed. If they are respected for their expertise, any resistance they pose will be a major hindrance to moving forward. More important, their objections may be well founded, and listening to them could prevent problems.

- *Thought Leader.* In any group there will be a few individual whose opinions help to galvanize the thinking of others who don't yet have an opinion. If the thought leaders believe the change is a good one, they can be useful in converting others and establishing positive momentum. If they resist the change, they can cause the momentum to swing in the other direction, in the process dragging out the time frame for implementation and multiplying the communications problems. A good strategy is to establish a rapport with the thought leaders and work them through the plan. If you get them to agree to give it a chance, it can make a significant difference in your effectiveness.

Ultimately the degree to which you communicate with those involved in a change situation will determine the quality of the implementation. Interacting is the best way to uncover which homeostatic factors are at work, as well as the roles that individuals will play. Underlying both of these concepts is the recognition that resistance to change is an emotional issue more than just a technical or operational one.

Matters of the Heart

Emotion and Change

In each stage of the change cycle, the actions that are taken have a varying impact on people's emotions. This goes beyond the concept of homeostasis. Resistance stems from the potential for change to tamper with some of the basic beliefs about the profession and the fundamental motivations for having chosen it. Since each change stage implies that movements in the environment may be the more significant issue for the organization, these movements can also signal adjustments in the core values of the entire industry or occupation.

Librarians who work in some large urban areas are experiencing this phenomenon. Those with degrees in library science may have chosen their career based on a love of books, a love of learning, and the satisfaction of assisting curious minds. Now, the increases in illiteracy, homelessness, latchkey kids, and reliance on the video medium have converged to produce some profound changes in their jobs. The pressure to come up with innovative programs to boost circulation or to reach out to new market segments can be refreshing or frustrating. The core values may be challenged because the customer is not the same one they thought they would be serving. The overall decline in reading directs their energies toward getting people interested in using the library to begin with.

In the Emerging stage, you will see this quite often—a change in direction may hinge on tampering with core values. In the Expanding stage, the realignment of processes and involvement of customers and suppliers in determining what quality is can cause resentment. It goes against the grain of many employees' beliefs about what influence outsiders should have on their professional judgment. For organizations in the Maturity stage that look to occupy new market niches, employees' belief systems may be confronted with the prospect of abandoning products or services that they have always felt were the backbone of the enterprise.

In the Entrenched stage, bold new leadership can threaten the professional values of employees by repositioning people. Finally, the Complex stage creates a twofold emotional impact: the shock treatment used to bring people to the conclusion that they cannot continue the way they are going, coupled with the recreation of the fundamental assumptions that have governed the organization, can produce intense emotional responses. There is an identifiable sequence of emotional response that can be applied to any stage. If understood, it can help you weather the storm.

The Emotional Response Sequence

The goal of understanding the sequence of emotional responses is *not* to limit the expression of those emotions. In fact, that can be one of the most dangerous things you can do. Feelings are a natural, normal, and necessary part of dealing with change. In some cases, the opportunity to vent frustrations, hostilities, or fears can actually assist the change process. Once people have had a chance to purge themselves, they can see and think more clearly. Attempting to stifle them will only increase the depth of emotion and prolong the process. Here are the key junctures in the sequence:

Sequence of Emotional Response

1. Inquiry
2. Denial
3. Pessimism
4. Education and analysis
5. Decision making
6. Action
7. Reaction
8. Acceptance

The **Inquiry** phase is that time before the particular change is actually made public. In most organizations, the grapevine functions to give people advance notice of decisions that have been made. In this phase employees are curious about the technical aspects of the proposed change but have not yet considered the impact. There is no real emotion here, but the stage is set for the direction of the subsequent phases.

Once a significant change does become public, the response may reflect **Denial.** People hear it but can't or don't want to believe it. This response can be predicated on any number of issues. The challenge to homeostasis or to the belief system may be too painful as people imagine how the change will alter basic facets of their life-style or work habits. A gatekeeper may think it's incredulous that management would attempt such a thing. Regardless of the source, most hope it's all a bad dream and things will return to normal when they wake up.

Pessimism will tend to be the immediate reaction when it becomes clear that the change will take place. There is something about human nature that leans toward the negative side of things. Employees will look at all of the downside risks of the implementation, without being able to consider the benefits. This is an important intervention point. Managers leading the change process have a tendency to shy away from these reactions or to become dictatorial in enforcing the plan. Here is the time to increase communication, interaction, and information sharing. The pessimism will abate more rapidly as people are supplied with information.

Employees will take it upon themselves to further their **Education** about the implications of the change. They will conduct extensive **Analysis** on everything from the general issues of the consistency of the change with the mission of the organization to specifics of how their own jobs will be affected. Here again, information can help reduce the degree of negativity and skepticism.

At some point, once all the data are in, there will be some **Decision Making** about "where they are" and what their position toward the change will be. The criterion for this decision is simply their feelings about the status quo relative to the proposed state. Figure 9-1 summarizes the possible outcomes.

Figure 9-1. Change response matrix.

		Proposed State	
		Approve	**Disapprove**
Status Quo	**Approve**	**Potential allies**	**Adversaries**
	Disapprove	**Ambassadors**	**Nay-sayers**

Once positional decisions have been made, the manager leading the change must be able to ascertain these positions in order to understand the nature of the **Action** that each will likely take. Potential Allies will be the silent force behind the scenes. However, if the overall resistance is high and these people are not thought of as leaders, it will be important to cultivate their support. Ambassadors are those whom you will want to invest in. If they are thought to be leaders, it bodes extremely well for the change, especially if they participate in the implementation planning.

The nay-sayers are just that—you don't know where they stand. Don't ignore this group. Their emotional response will either help or hinder; it will never be neutral. The Adversaries need to be cultivated as well. You can bet that some will never buy in. Don't let that be an excuse for not meeting with them and keeping them up to date. The key here is to cut your losses. Winning may not be possible, for if the overall resistance can be managed, it may not be enough to bring things to a halt. Ignoring this group encourages subversion, which can be detrimental to everyone.

Efforts to intervene at the action phase will cause **Reaction.** This is where you have an opportunity to bargain, negotiate, and collaborate with all involved to help satisfy their demands and needs. The objective is to craft a level of **Acceptance** that is not based solely on compliance, force, or fear. Such implementation of change may work on the surface, but inside there will be resentment that may come back to haunt you. Dealing with the emotional responses of those affected by the changes implemented is not easy, but is necessary. The time and energy required will be well worth it, as judged by the staying power and positive impact of the change itself. People have to go through turmoil; there is no easy way out. But there is a way. We are on the verge of a new order of the age in organizational life that will mandate that those in leadership positions take the time and personal energy to see that it is done as elegantly as possible.

The Balancing Act

It is impossible to define a single approach to managing change that captures all of the key requirements. We have been able to observe a number of skills, techniques, and insights that have the cumulative effect of producing the right results at the right time. These insights should also be useful in appreciating the big picture and dealing more artfully with the human beings who are involved. It is all one big balancing act, and we now stand on a challenging precipice where new things will be demanded of all of us.

New Models of Behavior and Conduct

At least the learning curve in dealing with change has been greatly accelerated, and we indeed see some hopeful signs. The cry of the workforce has gone up to the ears of management, and for once it seems they are actually hearing what is being said. Paradigms really are shifting. Whether through force or foresight, it's becoming increasingly clear to people in leadership that the expectations for their behavior and conduct are being altered.

There are new models for how people should be managed. In fact, there are many organizations undergoing reinvention who are throwing the concept of management itself out the window. Instead basic attributes, characteristics, and traits are being promoted as more appropriate for the organization of the future. Opinions vary on exactly how new these models really are. Some say we aren't asking anything more of managers and supervisors than we always have. The difference now is that we are insisting that they actually do what they are being paid to do. In other words, we have come up with new labels to describe what we have needed from them all along. Others feel that the insistence on performing those functions and the structural changes that are often required to make them operational is a new thing in and of itself.

Regardless of which side you line up with, the clear fact is that expectations are undergoing major revisions. Just what are these models, and how can we integrate them? There are numerous ways to consolidate the various ideas. They range from a very practical emphasis on coaching skills, to the implementation of self-managing teams, to the more nebulous emphasis on "visioning." Each has benefits and drawbacks, but taken collectively they do say something different about what we are proposing should be valued in the future.

If you were to aggregate all of them, you would see three major themes throughout: (1) *how to handle power*, with a decided emphasis on sharing it with those who usually don't get to; (2) *how to exhibit servanthood*, which speaks of redefinition of the job of a leader and the modus operandi that is employed; and (3) *how to restore connectedness in the work environment*, which posits that this sense of belonging is either missing or is needed in greater quantities. Overall, these attributes are interrelated and overlapping. They are methods to create an environment that will be conducive to managing greater degrees of change that will be coming at us at an even faster rate.

Handling Power

Fundamental to all human relations is the concept of power and authority. While we tend to shy away from too much focus on these, neither should be a dirty word. The fact that more often than not it is speaks volumes about the problem. Those who have power rarely want to share it. Our history reveals that normally when people get too much of it, it goes to their head, and they abuse the privileges that come with their position. Ultimately they abuse the people they are supposed to be leading, which is what gives power such a bad name. At the base of the impetus for revision is an insistence on a level of integrity that supersedes the desire and need to get ahead.

On a practical level, there are several different types of power, and leaders need to recognize them and know how to use each in the right way:

- Power that comes with title and position.
- Power because of the ability to dish out punishment or dole out rewards.
- Power because of competence and commitment to doing the job at the highest level of quality possible.
- Power because of a way of treating others that causes them to want to follow that leader.

The latter two types are becoming more valued. Training and development programs are being created to teach, reinforce, and motivate leaders to exhibit these attributes.

We refer often to the presence of politics in the organization. The technical definition of this word relates to the way that power is exchanged in a society. In essence, what is being suggested is that we can do a better job of dealing with the prospects of change if we put the power in the hands of those whose response to change is critical to our keeping balance as an organization. The feeling of powerlessness is viewed by many people at the working level as the most deflating and demotivating aspect of their jobs. Yet the mandate to redistribute power and authority must include exposing those who choose to exhibit oppressive behaviors as a primary way of interacting with their coworkers. These behaviors include activities as common as putting someone's request on the bottom of the pile to more dastardly deeds like sabotaging the work product of others to keep from being outdone. Certainly there are enough gray areas in organizational life and a need for checks and balances. But what I'm talking about here are the hidden agendas and covert planning that do no one any good—least of all the perpetrator. Confronting and eliminating these activities takes a lot of personal courage—perhaps more than the average person has at his or her disposal. How often have you encountered people in positions of authority who are too timid even to give you constructive feedback, much less be able to be directive?

Outside of the problems associated with the interpersonal side to this, there are other ways that the power is being passed around. There has been and likely will continue to be a trend toward employees' having a stake in the outcome of the organization's activities. Numerous Expanding-stage companies give workers a share of the cost savings that they can produce by working more efficiently. Others have become aggressive in implementing employee stock ownership.

Companies like the Saturn automobile maker combine the best of both worlds, mixing workplace autonomy and decision making with financial incentives. They have recognized that ownership is a lot broader than any one dimension. It's an attitude about who the powerful people are and what needs to take place for them to exercise their power for the good of the customers and, by logical extension, the company. Whether these responses come from the desperation to stay in business or from the decision to do things now that will keep the business in operation later can make all the difference in the world.

Exhibiting Servanthood

It used to be that the application of leadership could be confined to being good at giving instructions and making sure they were followed. Perhaps this will never vanish completely, but it is expected that a manager will learn to get the same results with a different style and approach. You might even want to begin using a word like *facilitator* to describe this style and approach. The word means literally "to make something easier." In that context, the leader of tomorrow will have to learn to serve those he or she leads.

You can immediately see the connection with the issue of handling power and dealing with change. Now the roles are reversed. Employees have been serving bosses for decades, and either they're tired of it and aren't going to take it any more or someone has reasoned correctly that this is a profound waste of time and talent. Perhaps it used to be that the boss actually knew more than anyone else and therefore "deserved" the deference. Today we find that it is frequently the other way around, as our examination of the Expanding-stage organization's use of the principles of managing quality revealed. At any stage, however, there is hardly any such gap in expertise, although we haven't stopped acting as if there is.

The act of servanthood has some practical elements to it. One is that leaders are learning to ask questions that bring out workers' knowledge and information rather than assume they alone have all of the answers. In a lot of organizations, asking question is a lost art, but when experience is increasingly less potent as a managerial tool, you have to be able to penetrate to the core of the matter. We've placed far too much emphasis on the experience of leaders and less on that of workers. What's worse is that in organizations that have thousands of employees (and/or are spread out over the expanse of the globe), there is no way to know what's happening even with all of the experience in the world.

I will never forget talking with the late W. Edwards Deming and his making reference to the CEO of one of the large automakers. This was a man Deming said he had known for years and greatly respected as a person. But with over thirty-odd years of experience in management and leadership, the man had not learned anything. All of the solutions that his background and training had encountered yielded few results in abating the pressures his company found itself confronted with. The business had changed, but he didn't know what questions to ask to evaluate how the company should change. He had not been able to move the organization further because his experience could not teach about the future.

Servanthood on another level speaks to the role of running interference for employees. The barriers between departments or work units can stifle productivity. Someone in a position of authority who wants to know how to help the average worker do his or her job will be welcomed with open arms by that person. In fact, the shock value of the offer is enough to add a boost of adrenaline to the motivational climate. It takes Tom Peters's "managing-by-walking-about" idea one step further. In the future when you walk about, you will have to do something other than conduct good public relations.

The drawbacks to this new model have more to do with working out the logistics than with whether it's useful. It's tough to change from Dr. No to Dr. Spock. For the untrained, implementation of servanthood may be nothing more than too much participative management, which is just as bad as too little. For the unwilling, implementation may be limited to empowering a few zealous workers in a few specific situations rather than actually turning over entire functions to the group. The self-managed team and coaching approach that is gaining popularity provides some of the key skills.

Self-managed teams are essentially an organizational system whereby the workers are given total control over the end product they are responsible for. This includes performing all of the technical and support functions that are needed. Most of these functions—personnel management, budgeting, scheduling, purchasing—would have been done by managers or supervisors, who now simply aren't needed. What is needed is someone who can coordinate, communicate with, and facilitate the operation of this system. Again, some say the skills to do this are the same ones we've always taught; others say the skill requirements are unique. Both are right to some degree.

It has always been a personal decision as to whether you were willing to be a servant, but when the team fills out *your* performance evaluation and decides if *your* raise will be forthcoming, this rating tends to get the attention of even the most recalcitrant. The intangible quality to servanthood is how to motivate without dire consequences. The supporters of approaches like self-managed teams know for sure what the benefits are to the team; but a challenge for the future will be to understand how to convey those benefits to the servant. There are some people who will gladly lay their lives down in order to bless those they lead. The trick is figuring out how to make it work for everyone else.

Restoring Connectedness

Here too the philosophical debate over motivation still rages. Behaviorists argue that the need to belong is legitimate and enduring; others don't debate that need but hold that the workplace is no longer seen as the place to have it satisfied. For many, the workplace is actually viewed as the problem. The inordinate amount of mental and physical time that parents spend at work, they say, has not helped the family unit at all. In addition, downsizing, streamlining, and flattening the hierarchy have eroded the confidence of even management. The sword of Damocles has always hovered over the heads of the line workers, but when the white-collar folks are forced to live in fear—well, that's another story.

On top of these we are finally beginning to address the root causes of prejudice, especially the volatile topics of sexism, racism, and other types of bigoted thinking. The process and outcome are good, but there is a short-term price to pay. After years of not being or feeling connected, employees are getting a chance to express themselves. After being pent up for so long, it will take a bit of time for the wounds to heal, if they can. Add to this an increase in the gender, ethnic, physical capability, and educational mix of the workplace overall, and it's clear that we have our work cut out for us.

The barriers that exist in the workplace between people who are different from one another are significant and cannot be underestimated. And if all of this isn't enough, we are adding to the categories that cover "being different." We never knew that so many people have been made to feel left out and denied a chance to participate fully and enjoy the access and privileges of the rest. No wonder productivity has suffered.

You can see the difficulty in trying to balance the role that connectedness plays in getting the work done with the fact that a lot of people don't want to be connected any more. The problems just mentioned, as well as other forces, have lowered the loyalty quotient among all categories of employee. Enter the new leader who must be a balm to the hurts of the past and prepare for the changes that are already upon us, never mind those that are to come. This is the one area where my personal skepticism shows. This takes special skills that are a rare commodity.

Nevertheless, the need is great. What has been noticeable is that when leaders do a good enough job handling power and exhibiting servanthood, they create the opportunity for dialogue. Honest communication about connectedness, or the lack thereof, is the common denominator in the organizations where some progress had been made. Organizations that can at least establish the boundaries for how people will be treated inside can ward off the encroachment from the outside. After all, prejudice of whatever variety is a larger problem of our society and automatically gets brought into the workplace.

Leaders of tomorrow will manage change successfully only if they can make clear that such behaviors (and possibly even attitudes) have no place inside the organization, regardless of how one chooses to conduct themselves elsewhere. Continuing education on the nature of cultural differences, based on the broadest possible definition of culture, will be the hallmark of the successful organization. The courage to sit down and talk about interpersonal problems rather than just give them a convenient label will exemplify the character of the successful person.

A Final Word

We have covered a lot of territory and viewed much of the terrain concerning managing change. I hope the objectivity will serve you well as you try to make use of the concepts, techniques, and skills. Perhaps one of life's greatest lessons can be applied as a closing thought and that is this idea of balance. Edwin Louis Cole says that "balance is the key to life." It may also be the key to dealing with organizational change.

We in positions of authority and responsibility tend to make the most expensive mistakes when we lose sight of the concept of balance. We plan for the future without enough attention to the details of today. We enforce standards and rules without tempering them with grace. We increase our share of the market and lose the human touch. We focus on the value of being able to lead and forget what it is like to follow. In all of these things, balance will preserve us. No matter how much change we incur or how much change we ourselves create, if we can remember to consider what will be best for all involved, our errors will be fewer, our satisfaction greater, and our sleep that much more filled with peace.

The future awaits us. Let us not tarry.

Index